Test Your I.Q.

by

Alfred W. Munzert, Ph.D.

Prentice Hall
New York • London • Toronto • Sydney • Tokyo • Singapore

I would like to acknowledge the invaluable contribution of Mary Colvin, whose many hours of research and professional assistance have helped to make this book possible.

Third Edition

 Prentice Hall General Reference
15 Columbus Circle
New York, NY 10023

An Arco Book

ARCO and PRENTICE HALL are registered trademarks
of Prentice-Hall, Inc.
Colophon is a trademark of Prentice-Hall, Inc.

Manufactured in the United States of America

1   2   3   4   5   6   7   8   9   10

Library of Congress Cataloging-in-Publication Data

Munzert, Alfred W.
  Test your I.Q. / by Alfred W. Munzert. -- 3rd ed.
      p.   cm.
  Includes bibliographical references.
  ISBN 0-671-87459-4
    1. Intelligence tests. 2. Self-evaluation. I. Title
BF431.M823   1994
153.9'33—dc20   93-39956
                                              CIP

Contents

	Page
Introduction	iv
Part I: SELF-SCORING I.Q. TEST	1
Instructions	3
I.Q. Test	7
Answers and Explanations	17
Scoring Instructions	21
Part II: INTELLIGENCE: ITS MEASUREMENT AND MEANING	23
Measuring Intelligence	25
Your Intelligence Score (I.Q.)	28
Intelligence: What Is It?	32
Differences in Child and Adult Intelligence	37
Brain Function: Creativity and Intelligence	42
The Significance of Right-Brain Intelligence to the Educational System and National Achievement	46
Methodology for Teaching Right-Brain Dominated People	50
I.Q. Test Analysis: Left-Brain, Right-Brain Abilities	54
Left-Brain, Right-Brain Test Analysis	62
Creativity	63
Are Intelligence Scores Useful and Important?	70
Can Intelligence Be Improved or Raised?	76
Part III: GIFTEDNESS/TALENT AND INTELLIGENCE	83
Observing for Indicators of Giftedness and Talent	84
Milestones in Infant and Preschool Development	89
Checklist of Behaviors to Measure Giftedness and Talent	92
Summary	100
Part IV: COMPUTER I.Q.	101
Intelligence and Computer Operation	102
Computer Operator Test	104
Answers and Explanations	118
Test Interpretation	123

Introduction

OF ALL the subjects that intrigue our modern society, none is more fascinating than intelligence. Specifically, what do we mean by intelligence? How is it measured? Of even greater importance—what are the implications of such measurement to the individual?

Far more than idle curiosity prompts such questions. Not only is our educational system structured to channel the intelligence of the individual into desired and productive behaviors, but the entire society tends to create a hierarchy of status and reward based upon the perceived intelligence of its members. For the individual, who must cope with this complexity, the desire to know more about his or her intelligence and abilities is not just compelled by ego—it is vital knowledge that can impact every facet of existence. It is the purpose of this book to present not only an instrument for the measurement of the intelligence quotient (I.Q.), but also other significant information regarding human intelligence that will be of value to the reader. If this book assists the reader to a more profound self-understanding and analysis of his or her ability to cope with the surrounding society, then it will have fulfilled its objective.

Alfred W. Munzert, Ph.D.

I

Self-Scoring I.Q. Test

Answer Sheet
for I.Q. Test

Before you begin the I.Q. Test on page 7, tear out this page and place it beside your book.

Write the letter or number of your answer choice on the line beside the question number.

1.	_____	21.	_____	41.	_____
2.	_____	22.	_____	42.	_____
3.	_____	23.	_____	43.	_____
4.	_____	24.	_____	44.	_____
5.	_____	25.	_____	45.	_____
6.	_____	26.	_____	46.	_____
7.	_____	27.	_____	47.	_____
8.	_____	28.	_____	48.	_____
9.	_____	29.	_____	49.	_____
10.	_____	30.	_____	50.	_____
11.	_____	31.	_____	51.	_____
12.	_____	32.	_____	52.	_____
13.	_____	33.	_____	53.	_____
14.	_____	34.	_____	54.	_____
15.	_____	35.	_____	55.	_____
16.	_____	36.	_____	56.	_____
17.	_____	37.	_____	57.	_____
18.	_____	38.	_____	58.	_____
19.	_____	39.	_____	59.	_____
20.	_____	40.	_____	60.	_____

Instructions

On the following pages, you will take a carefully constructed test designed to measure your intelligence. You may take this test if you are eleven years or older. Take the test only when you are in a fresh state of mind. Be sure that your testing conditions include good lighting and a quiet, comfortable work area. Please carefully observe the time restrictions and do not discuss the questions with anyone else while taking the test.

At the end of the test, you will find a complete scoring table and explanations of the answers to all of the questions. The explanations will help you understand the basis of the test. Later sections of this book will include a detailed discussion of how the test is scored and interpreted and of how I.Q. is measured. You will also find an important discussion of left-brain and right-brain functions and their relationship to intelligence scores. Although the test itself will give you a fairly accurate index of your intelligence, there are many other aspects of the human intellect—such as creativity, musical talent, and psychomotor skills—that are *not* measured by an I.Q. test. These are carefully explored in the other sections of this book. We strongly recommend that you review each of these in order to gain a complete understanding of human intelligence.

IMPORTANT!
Read These Instructions First

A. Instructions

1. You have 45 minutes to answer the 60 questions. Do *not* exceed this time limit.

2. Answer *all* questions. If you do not know the answer—guess. Guessing has been considered in the scoring. Do not leave any question unanswered.

3.   If a question seems to have more than one answer or no correct answer at all, pick what you consider to be the *best* of the choices given. These questions are purposely designed to test your ability to think and reason.

B. Sample Questions

Carefully study the following sample questions before beginning the test.

I.   In some questions you will be asked to make a comparison.

EXAMPLE: Which one of the five makes the best comparison?

Boat is to water as airplane is to:
SUN—GROUND—WATER—SKY—TREE

The answer is *sky*. A boat travels through water. This can be compared to an airplane that travels through the sky.

You will also be asked to compare designs.

EXAMPLE: Which one of the five makes the best comparison?

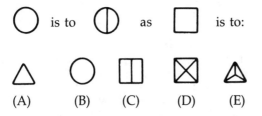

The answer is C. A circle that is divided into two parts can be compared to a square that is also divided into two parts.

II. In some questions you will be given a group of five things. Four of them will have something in common; they will be similar in some way. You will be asked to choose the one that is not similar to the other four.

EXAMPLE: Which one of the five is least like the other four?

DOG—CAR—CAT—BIRD—FISH

The answer is *car*. The others are all living creatures. A car is not alive.
These questions may also be based on designs.

EXAMPLE: Which one of the five is least like the other four?

(A)   (B)   (C)   (D)   (E)

The answer is D. The others are all made with straight lines. A circle is a curved line.

III. In some questions you will be given numbers or letters which are in a certain order. They follow some pattern of arrangement. However, one of them will not fit. You will be asked to choose the one that does not fit into the pattern.

EXAMPLE: Which one of the numbers does not belong in the following series?

1—3—5—7—9—10—11—13

The answer is 10. Starting with 1, the odd numbers are arranged in order; 10 is an even number, which does not fit in the series.

IV.   There will also be some problems which you will be asked to solve. These will not require any difficult math. Instead, they will be testing how logical you are—that is, how well you think.

You are now ready to begin the test. Read each question carefully and write the letter of your answer or the number that you choose in the space next to the question number on the answer sheet on page 2. Tear out the answer sheet before you begin. You have 45 minutes to answer the questions.

I.Q. Test

1. Which of the five makes the best comparison?

YYZZZYZZY is to 221112112 as YYZZYZZY is to:

221221122	22112122	22112112	112212211	212211212
(a)	(b)	(c)	(d)	(e)

2. Which of the five is least like the other four?

NICKEL	TIN	STEEL	IRON	COPPER
(a)	(b)	(c)	(d)	(e)

3. Which of the five designs makes the best comparison?

(a)	(b)	(c)	(d)	(e)

4. Which of the five designs is least like the other four?

(a)	(b)	(c)	(d)	(e)

5. Jerry received both the 15th highest and the 15th lowest mark in the class. How many students are in the class?

15	25	29	30	32
(a)	(b)	(c)	(d)	(e)

6. Which of the five is least like the other four?

DICTIONARY	BIOGRAPHY	ATLAS	ALMANAC	DIRECTORY
(a)	(b)	(c)	(d)	(e)

7

7. Which of the five is least like the other four?

A Z F N H

(a)   (b)   (c)   (d)   (e)

8. Which of the five makes the best comparison?

Foot is to hand as leg is to:

ELBOW	PIANO	TOE	FINGER	ARM
(a)	(b)	(c)	(d)	(e)

9. Which of the five designs makes the best comparison?

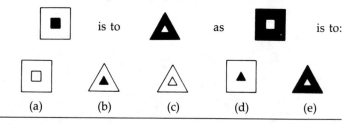

(a)   (b)   (c)   (d)   (e)

10. If all Ferpies are Worgs and no Worgs are Sprikles, then no Sprikles are definitely Ferpies.

This statement is definitely:

TRUE	FALSE	NEITHER
(a)	(b)	(c)

11. Of the following numbers, which one is least like the others?

1   3   5   7   11   13   15   17   19

12. Which of the five designs is least like the other four?

(a)   (b)   (c)   (d)   (e)

13. Terry is older than Mark and Sam is younger than Terry.

Which of the following statements is most accurate?

(a) Sam is older than Mark.

(b) Sam is younger than Mark.

(c) Sam is as old as Mark.

(d) It is impossible to tell whether Sam or Mark is older.

14. Which of the five designs is least like the other four?

    (a)   (b)   (c)   (d)   (e)

15. Which of the five makes the best comparison?

Leap is to peal as 8326 is to:

2368	6283	2683	6328	3628
(a)	(b)	(c)	(d)	(e)

16. Anne received $.59 change from a supermarket purchase. Of the eleven coins she received in change, three were exactly alike. These three coins had to be:

PENNIES	NICKELS	DIMES	QUARTERS	HALF DOLLARS
(a)	(b)	(c)	(d)	(e)

17. Which of the five is least like the other four?

PECK	OUNCE	PINT	CUP	QUART
(a)	(b)	(c)	(d)	(e)

18. Three enemy messages were intercepted at communications head-quarters. The code was broken and it was found that "Berok tenlis krux" means "Secret attack Wednesday" and "Baroom zax Tenlis" means "Secret plans included" and "Gradnor berok plil elan" means "Wednesday victory is ours." What does "krux" mean?

SECRET	WEDNESDAY	NOTHING	ATTACK	PLANS
(a)	(b)	(c)	(d)	(e)

19. Which of the five makes the best comparison?

Love is to hate as valor is to:

COURAGE	SECURITY	COWARDICE	ANGER	TERROR
(a)	(b)	(c)	(d)	(e)

20. The price of an article was cut 50% for a sale. By what percent must the item be increased to again sell at the original price?

25%	50%	75%	100%	200%
(a)	(b)	(c)	(d)	(e)

21. Which of the five designs makes the best comparison?

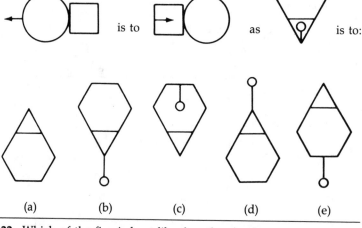

(a)	(b)	(c)	(d)	(e)

22. Which of the five is least like the other four?

SQUASH	PUMPKIN	TOMATO	CUCUMBER	CORN
(a)	(b)	(c)	(d)	(e)

23. Which of the five makes the best comparison?

Hole is to doughnut as pages are to:

STORY	WORDS	CONTENTS	INDEX	COVER
(a)	(b)	(c)	(d)	(e)

24. Kim was sent to the store to get eleven large cans of fruit. Kim could carry only 2 cans at a time. How many trips to the store did Kim have to make?

5	5½	6	6½	7
(a)	(b)	(c)	(d)	(e)

25. Which of the five designs makes the best comparison?

(a)	(b)	(c)	(d)	(e)

26. If all Pleeps are Floops and all Floops are Leepies, then all Pleeps are definitely Leepies.

This statement is definitely:

TRUE	FALSE	NEITHER
(a)	(b)	(c)

27. Which of the five designs is least like the other four?

X	T	N	V	L
(a)	(b)	(c)	(d)	(e)

28. Jim, John, Jerry, and Joe together bought a basket of 144 apples. Jim received 10 more apples than John, 26 more than Jerry, and 32 more than Joe.

How many apples did Jim receive?

73	63	53	43	27
(a)	(b)	(c)	(d)	(e)

29. Which of the five is least like the other four?

TOUCH	SEE	HEAR	EAT	SMELL
(a)	(b)	(c)	(d)	(e)

30. Which of the five makes the best comparison?

Daughter is to father as niece is to:

NEPHEW	COUSIN	UNCLE	MOTHER	BROTHER
(a)	(b)	(c)	(d)	(e)

31. Which of the five designs is least like the other four?

| (a) | (b) | (c) | (d) | (e) |

32. Which number does not belong in the following series?

4   5   8   10   11   16   19   32   36

33. Which of the five makes the best comparison?

Bark is to tree as scales are to:

GILLS	ELEPHANT	BUTCHER	FISH	SKIN
(a)	(b)	(c)	(d)	(e)

34. Which of the five is least like the other four?

TURKEY	DUCK	CHICKEN	PHEASANT	GOOSE
(a)	(b)	(c)	(d)	(e)

35. The secher vlooped quaply berak the kriggly lool. Then the secher _____ flaxly down the kleek.

Which word belongs in the space?

VLOOPED	QUAPLY	BERAK	LOOL	KRIGGLY
(a)	(b)	(c)	(d)	(e)

36. The fish has a head 9 inches long. The tail is equal to the size of the head plus one half the size of the body. The body is the size of the head plus the tail. How long is the fish?

27 inches	54 inches	63 inches	72 inches	81 inches
(a)	(b)	(c)	(d)	(e)

37. Which of the five designs is least like the other four?

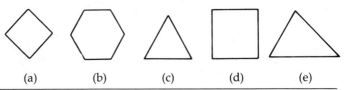

(a)	(b)	(c)	(d)	(e)

38. If you rearrange the letters in "NAICH," you would have the name of a(n):

COUNTRY	OCEAN	STATE	CITY	ANIMAL
(a)	(b)	(c)	(d)	(e)

39. Jack is 15 years old, three times as old as his sister. How old will Jack be when he is twice as old as his sister?

18	20	24	26	30
(a)	(b)	(c)	(d)	(e)

40. Which of the five designs makes the best comparison?

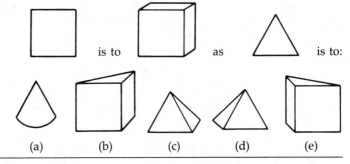

(a)	(b)	(c)	(d)	(e)

41. Slok are more zitful than mulk, but pringling flex are most _____ of all.

Which word belongs in the blank space?

SLOK	ZITFUL	MULK	PRINGLING	FLEZ
(a)	(b)	(c)	(d)	(e)

42. Which of the five makes the best comparison?

is to   as   is to:

(a)   (b)   (c)   (d)   (e)

43. If you rearrange the letters in "SHORE," you would have the name of a(n):

COUNTRY	OCEAN	STATE	CITY	ANIMAL
(a)	(b)	(c)	(d)	(e)

44. Which number does not belong in the following series?

1   3   5   7   9   11   12   13   15

45. Which of the five makes the best comparison?

Gas is to car as food is to:

MOUTH	STOMACH	ENERGY	BODY	TEETH
(a)	(b)	(c)	(d)	(e)

46. Which of the five designs is least like the other four?

(a)   (b)   (c)   (d)   (e)

47. Which of the five is least like the other four?

WICHITA	DALLAS	CANTON	BANGOR	FRESNO
(a)	(b)	(c)	(d)	(e)

48. If some Tripples are Tropples and all Bolars are Tropples, then some Tripples are definitely Bolars.

This statement is:

TRUE	FALSE	NEITHER
(a)	(b)	(c)

49. Which of the five designs makes the best comparison?

50. Which of the five makes the best comparison?

Sack is to sad as turn is to:

TACK	UP	TURF	BURN	TOY
(a)	(b)	(c)	(d)	(e)

51. Which of the five designs is least like the other four?

52. Which letter does not belong in the following series?

B   E   H   K   M   N   Q   T

53. Which of the five makes the best comparison?

Pillow is to pillowcase as arm is to:

BODY	SLEEVE	HAND	GLOVE	RING
(a)	(b)	(c)	(d)	(e)

54. Which of the five is least like the other four?

(a)   (b)   (c)   (d)   (e)

55. Which of the five is least like the other four?

(a)   (b)   (c)   (d)   (e)

56. If all Truples are Glogs and some Glogs are Glips, then some Truples are definitely Glips.

This statement is:

TRUE	FALSE	NEITHER
(a)	(b)	(c)

57. If you rearrange the letters in "TALCATIN" you would have the name of a:

COUNTRY	OCEAN	STATE	CITY	ANIMAL
(a)	(b)	(c)	(d)	(e)

58. Which of the five is least like the other four?

ARTIST	GOLFER	NEWSCASTER	DANCER	MECHANIC
(a)	(b)	(c)	(d)	(e)

59. Which of the five does not belong in the series?

(a)   (b)   (c)   (d)   (e)

60. Which of the five is least like the other four?

WATER	SUN	GASOLINE	WIND	CEMENT
(a)	(b)	(c)	(d)	(e)

Answers and Explanations

1. **C** Substitute numbers for letters: Y = 2; Z = 1.

2. **C** (steel) The others are simple metals; steel is an alloy (combination of two metals).

3. **A** The six-sided hexagon is divided into six equal parts by lines drawn from its outside vertices, just as the three-sided triangle is divided into three equal parts by lines drawn from its outside vertices.

4. **C** All the others are made with three lines; V is made with two lines.

5. **C** There are 14 students higher and 14 students lower. Jerry is the 29th student; the one in the middle.

6. **B** All the others are reference books. A biography is a narrative.

7. **A** The others are consonants; A is a vowel.

8. **E** A foot is attached to a leg; a hand is attached to an arm.

9. **B** The square changes to a triangle and the shading is reversed.

10. **A** Example: If all dogs are animals and no animals are plants, then no plants are definitely dogs.

11. **15** The others are prime numbers—they can only be divided by themselves and 1. Fifteen is not a prime number. It can be divided by itself, 1, 3, and 5.

12. **C** The others are all made from a straight line and a curve. C is only a curve.

13. **D** Without more information it is impossible to tell. We only know that both Mark and Sam are younger than Terry.

14. **C** It is made with only straight lines. The others are made with straight lines and curves.

15. **D** Substitute numbers for letters: L = 8, E = 3, A = 2, P = 6. Peal = 6328.

16. **B**   Four dimes, three nickels, and four pennies is the only solution.

17. **A**   Peck is the only one which is a dry measure; the others measure both liquid and dry quantities.

18. **D**   tenlis = secret; berok = Wednesday; krux = attack

19. **C**   Love is the opposite of hate. Valor is the opposite of cowardice.

20. **D**   Example: A $20.00 item cut 50% will sell for $10.00. To again sell for $20.00, the item must be increased $10.00, which is 100% of $10.00.

21. **E**   The position of the geometric figures is reversed. The line figuration remains on the same side of the configuration, but is reversed.

22. **E**   Corn. The others grow on vines. Corn grows on a stalk.

23. **E**   The hole is inside the doughnut and the pages are inside the cover.

24. **C**   11/2 = 5½. It takes 6 trips; a half trip won't get the last can home.

25. **E**   It is a comparison of the same figure, solid to broken line.

26. **A**   Example: "If all dogs are mammals and all mammals are animals, then all dogs are definitely animals."

27. **C**   All the others are made with two lines; N is made with three lines.

28. **C**   Jim received 53; John received 53 − 10 or 43; Jerry received 53 − 26 or 27; Joe received 53 − 32 or 21. 53 + 43 + 27 + 21 = 144. This problem may be solved algebraically as well.

29. **D**   The others are senses; eating is a body function.

30. **C**   Daughter is the female child of father; niece is the female child of uncle.

31. **B**   All the other large figures have a smaller figure inside, which is same as the outside figure.

32. **11** The order is plus one, double the first figure; plus two, double the third figure; plus three, double the fifth figure; plus four.

33. **D** Bark is on the outside of a tree; scales are on the outside of a fish.

34. **D** The others are or can be domesticated; pheasant is wild.

35. **A** A verb must go in the space. Example: The teacher *walked* quickly toward the open door. Then the teacher *walked* quickly down the hall.

36. **D** The head is 9 inches. The tail is 18 inches + 9 inches = 27 inches. The body is 9 inches + 18 inches + 9 inches = 36 inches. 9 inches + 27 inches + 36 inches = 72 inches. This may be solved algebraically as well.

37. **E** All the other figures are symmetrical.

38. **A** "NAICH" = "CHINA."

39. **B** Jack is ten years older than his sister. In five years Jack will be 20, and his sister who is now 5 will be 10.

40. **C** The square is a direct frontal view of the cube that is seen looking from right to left. The triangle is a direct frontal view of the pyramid seen looking from right to left.

41. **B** An adverb is required. Example: Nickels are more *valuable* than pennies, but twenty dollars are most *valuable* of all.

42. **C** A person uses a pencil for the purpose of writing; a person uses the eye for the purpose of reading.

43. **E** "SHORE" = "HORSE."

44. **12** The series is made from counting by twos.

45. **D** Gas provides energy for a car; food provides energy for a body.

46. **B** All the others have an odd number of squares; B has an even number.

47. **A** All the others have but six letters; Wichita has seven.

48. **B** Example: "If some cars are green and all leaves are green, then some cars are definitely leaves."

49. **E** Four figures change into four figures. Six figures change into six figures.

50. **B** *Sad* can be combined with *sack* to make the word "sad-sack." *Up* can be combined with *turn* to make the word "upturn."

51. **A** It does not have a twin.

52. **M** The series is made up of every fourth letter of the alphabet, starting with B.

53. **B** A pillow fits inside a pillowcase. An arm fits inside a sleeve.

54. **B** All the others hold something inside. The cap fits on top of a head.

55. **C** The others all show mathematical relationships. + is a mathematical operation.

56. **B** Example: "If all cats are animals and some animals are dogs, then some cats are definitely dogs."

57. **B** "TALCATIN" = "ATLANTIC."

58. **C** All the others must use their hands and/or body but not words to perform their jobs. The newscaster must use words.

59. **D** The others have a sequence of letters in alphabetical order starting at the top and going clockwise.

60. **E** The others can all be used as sources of energy.

Scoring Instructions

Count up the number of questions that you answered correctly. Find that number in the column appropriate to your age and circle the number. Then, directly to the right in the I.Q. column you will locate your correct I.Q. rating. For example, if you are 14 years old and had 32 answers correct, you locate 32 in the 14-year-old column and find that you have an I.Q. rating of 114.

AGE						I.Q.
11	12	13	14	15	16+ Adult	
8	10	13	15	17	19	80
9	11	14	16	18	20	82
10	12	15	17	19	21	84
11	13	16	18	20	22	86
12	14	17	19	21	23	88
13	15	18	20	22	24	90
14	16	19	21	23	25	92
15	17	20	22	24	26	94
16	18	21	23	25	27	96
17	19	22	24	26	28	98
18	20	23	25	27	29	100
19	21	24	26	28	30	102
20	22	25	27	29	31	104
21	23	26	28	30	32	106
22	24	27	29	31	33	108
23	25	28	30	32	34	110
24	26	29	31	33	35	112
25	27	30	32	34	36	114
26	28	31	33	35	37	116

AGE						I.Q.
11	**12**	**13**	**14**	**15**	**16 + Adult**	
27	29	32	34	36	38	118
28	30	33	35	37	39	120
29	31	34	36	38	40	122
30	32	35	37	39	41	124
31	33	36	38	40	42	126
32	34	37	39	41	43	128
33	35	38	40	42	44	130
34	36	39	41	43	45	132
35	37	40	42	44	46	134
36	38	41	43	45	47	136
37	39	42	44	46	48	138
38	40	43	45	47	49	140
39	41	44	46	48	50	142
40	42	45	47	49	51	144
41	43	46	48	50	52	146
42	44	47	49	51	53	148
43	45	48	50	52	54	150
44	46	49	51	53	55	154
45	47	50	52	54	56	158
46	48	51	53	55	57	160
47	49	52	54	56	58 +	165 +

Intelligence: Its Measurement and Meaning

Measuring Intelligence

The measurement of intelligence has traditionally been put into the same category as top-secret, classified government information. I.Q. scores have been cloaked in a mystery of psychological terminology and ownership, and the general public has been left in awe of the idea and in ignorance of the results of individual testing. A certain amount of professional discretion is justified, as the results obtained from one or a set of individual intelligence tests need to be evaluated and interpreted within a context of many other facets of individual and group behavior.

In the more enlightened climate of recent times, people have the right to know their own and their children's I.Q. test scores. It would be a serious breach of professional responsibility, however, to indiscriminately disclose these scores either to parents or to children. Children are generally unequipped with the necessary knowledge, maturity, and experience to be able to understand or to respond to the meaning of I.Q. scores. Parents, while entitled to know, are also entitled to a full explanation of what their children's I.Q.s mean within the context of the learning environment, behavior, and achievement.

A knowledge of one's I.Q. has many advantages. Within the process of human development, an understanding of one's own potential and one's own limitations can be of enormous personal value. We all have both upward potential and personal limitations; I.Q. is but one of many indicators of both of these. It is important to know and to understand that many other factors come into play and are important to success and happiness. Motivation, sensitivity, industriousness, and capacity for love are among those factors and are among the abilities not measured by standard intelligence tests. Intelligence *per se* is important only if used and applied to the life tasks that confront an individual each day.

There is no real mystery to the measurement of intelligence. Essentially, any test with a large number of questions and problems that requires a person to use different intellectual skills to arrive at answers can be used to generate a test of intelligence. A test that provides questions that tap areas of perception, spatial awareness, language ability, numerical ability, and memory, and that requires a person to use comparisons, sequencing, classification, computation, problem-solving methods, comprehension, association, completion, reasoning, logic, analogy, evaluation, judgment, etc., in various content areas can be refined into a test of intelligence.

The test that you just took is a paper and pencil test typical of those given either to a single individual or to a group of persons at the same sitting. In addition to paper and pencil tests that use the preceding kinds of materials for questions, there are also individual I.Q. tests, given on a one-to-one basis, that include "performance" kinds of problem situations. Individual tests allow for testing of nonreaders or for testing of people who have difficulty with reading or with the language. Individual tests may test auditory and retentive skills by requiring the person being tested to listen to a sequence of numbers and then to repeat that sequence. Other performance items may include puzzle completion and block structure replication. These tend to test abilities not measured by paper and pencil tests, such as the motor skills that relate to mechanics and to the fine arts media. People who solve problems through pictures, objects, and emotions rather than by using numerical and language concepts are candidates for individual testing. These people often have a high degree of intelligence that cannot be measured with the more economical, traditional language-oriented paper and pencil type of test.

Intelligence tests do not measure creativity, although certain creative skills may be brought into play in order to successfully solve specific problems. The nature of creativity and its relationship to intelligence will be discussed later.

If you had picked up a book on intelligence published twenty-five or more years ago, the chances are that creativity would not have been discussed, at least not in any great detail. This is because creativity was associated with high performance in the visual and performing arts and was not considered an integral part of the behaviors associated with intelligence. However, research that has been conducted since the late 1950s, along with observations based upon experience, has shed new light upon the nature of creativity and its relationship to performance in all areas of human endeavor. In the next chapter, we shall explore the entire range of intelligence in order to give you a fuller understanding of its meaning and its measurement.

Your Intelligence Score (I.Q.)

Now that you have taken the intelligence test at the beginning of this book, you must be curious to know the meaning of your score or I.Q. Rest assured that you are indeed intelligent. Two indicators of intelligent behavior are *curiosity* and *language* or *reading ability*. Without these two qualities, you would not even be reading this book. Where you stand in relation to other people can be explained quite simply. The following graph shows how intelligence is distributed among the general population.

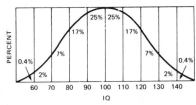

Distribution of Intelligence in the General Population

The above graph shows what is called a classical bell-shaped curve. It is based on laws of probability that test out in actual life. Most people have test scores or I.Q.s that fall into the middle of the curve. This means that average intelligence is found in approximately 50% of the population and ranges between an I.Q. of 90 and 110, with a score of 100 being the "magic" number of average intelligence.

The test score, or I.Q., stands for Intelligence Quotient. It is a specific numerical measurement of a less-than-specific concept—intelligence. Although I.Q. is an indicator of innate ability and potential, it is not a pure measure. Even the best test of innate ability is contaminated by specific ability factors and by information and skills gained through experience and learning. Nonetheless, I.Q. is a reasonably good descriptive and predictive measure. I.Q., or Intelligence Quotient, is computed by the following mathematical formula:

$$I.Q. = \frac{mental\ age}{chronological\ age} \times 100$$

Chronological age, of course, is actual age in years. Mental age is a construct based on test responses. Test questions are scientifically analyzed and determinations are made as to which problems a person of a certain age can be expected to answer successfully. After considerable statistical analysis, tests are "normed" or "standardized" by checking the actual number of correct answers given, for example, by a 10-year-old to the items considered as being the kind of problems an average 10-year-old should be able to successfully complete. If a 10-year-old takes the test and correctly completes the items a 10-year-old should be able to do, but no more, that indicates a mental age of 10. The formula is worked as follows:

$$I.Q. = \frac{10}{10}\ (or\ 1) \times 100$$

$$I.Q. = 100$$

If, however, a 10-year-old takes the test and completes not only the items that a 10-year-old should be able to do but also all the items that a 13-year-old should be able to do, that individual has a mental age of 13, and the formula is worked as follows:

$$I.Q. = \frac{13}{10}\ (or\ 1.3) \times 100$$

$$I.Q. = 130$$

If a 10-year-old takes the test but can only complete all the items that an average 8-year-old should be able to do, the mental age is 8 and the formula is worked as follows:

$$I.Q. = \frac{8}{10}\ (or\ 0.8) \times 100$$

$$I.Q. = 80$$

As already stated, the average I.Q. is between 90 and 110. A score between 110 and 119 indicates bright intelligence. A score between 120 and 129 indicates superior intelligence. A score of 130 or over is indicative of giftedness. However, some tests vary slightly, and intellectual giftedness might be shown in a score of 135 and above, or 140 and above.

Those persons who score over 160 are endowed with superior giftedness, often described as being in the "genius" category. However, the critical factor of intelligence is its development and use. Without development, application, and productivity, high intelligence is a valueless characteristic, both to the individual and to society.

An individual who scores between 80 and 89 is usually considered a slow learner. Scores under 80 indicate varying degrees of mental handicaps. However, these interpretations are made in relation to the person's *exhibited* abilities as measured on the test and their relationship to the abilities necessary for successful learning in a regular school situation. There are many reasons why I.Q., particularly the results of *one* test, may not indicate a true level of intelligence and potential capability. It is because of this that one I.Q. test score should never be used to label and place an individual in a permanent school or life setting. Even a pattern of scores should be evaluated against such other factors as behavior, interest, thinking style, and actual production.

For I.Q. scores to be most meaningful and helpful to those working with the individuals involved, it is best that a pattern of test scores be established over a period of time. This is one reason why it is important for youngsters to be present each time the test is administered in school. There are many reasons why the pattern of scores is important.

Scores will normally vary somewhat on different occasions and among different tests. There should, however, be an exhibited range of scores within about a 20-point variation. Reasons for this normal range of variation result from the following facts:

1. There are some differences in the tests themselves.

2. Differences in testing conditions will influence an individual's performance on tests at different times.

3.   Tests that are given to groups may be less accurate than tests that are individually given.

4.   The physical and mental well-being of the person taking the test will vary from one time to another.

A variation of more than 20 points is often an indication that more careful observation and/or testing needs to be conducted. For example, an extreme downward variation in test scores may indicate possible physical and/or psychological problems that require further investigation. An extreme upward variation suggests an upward limit of abilities that has gone undetected and therefore unmet and unchallenged, particularly in a formal school setting. In either case, additional testing and evaluation need to be carried out to determine which range of scores is most valid.

Intelligence: What Is It?

The word "intelligence" is so frequently used by both professionals and laymen that its meaning is taken for granted, couched somewhere in the context of how it is used. However, it is not a concept that is easy to define. Even among professionals, there is no one definition that explains the "attributes" of intelligence. That is because the word "intelligence" is a noun—a part of speech used to signify a thing or object which does have definite characteristics or descriptors. Intelligence is a highly complex or abstract "thing" for which there are no such definite attributes as long or short, red or green, light or heavy. When intelligence is studied or measured, what actually is observed is intelligent behavior or intelligent performance, not intelligence *per se*.

If we think in terms of intelligent behavior, rather than intelligence, it is easier to identify and build a basis for defining the abstract concept. For example, of the two behaviors shown below, check the one which you think is more intelligent.

ACTOR A   ACTOR B

Of course you checked the panel showing Actor B, whose behavior is far more intelligent than that of Actor A. You compared one behavior to a related behavior under the same set of circumstances. In order to do this, you had to have a basic storehouse of information about electricity, its nature, and its relationship to water. The process that you went through to make an observation and judgment of intelligent behavior should in itself give you some insight into the nature of intelligent behavior.

The basis of intelligent behavior must be some kind of knowledge and information in its broadest sense. This information may have been acquired formally or informally. For example, if Actor A were only two years old, the behavior shown would not be considered unintelligent on the part of the child. (We might question the intelligence of the parent who permitted the child to be in a position to act dangerously and without the information on which to act intelligently.)

The impact of intelligence upon intelligent behavior begins with memory. For instance, in the preceding example, information about electricity and the dangers of mixing electricity with water must be remembered in order to affect behavior.

A factor related to remembering information is the application of previous learning to current situations. This is the ability to transfer or to generalize. Some individuals have much more capacity for transfer than others. Persons well-endowed with this ability are usually found to be significantly more intelligent than those who do not possess a high degree of this ability.

Other facets of intelligence and intelligent behavior include speed in arriving at answers and solutions and problem-solving ability. To arrive at a solution, a person must identify the problem, analyze it, think of alternatives, apply previous knowledge, make a decision, and offer a solution. The entire act involves integration—putting it all together with balance and effficiency.

This essentially summarizes the nature of intelligent behavior. Intelligence tests try to measure intelligence by setting up situations and observing intelligent behavior. The tests use different kinds of questions and problems requiring the application of related and overlapping abilities. The various specialized tasks of the intelligence tests require an interplay of overall general ability and specific abilities in varying degrees. Intelligence tests must include a wide variety of question types in order to come up with a single score. As we continue to use the term "intelligence" in this context, it is important to understand that we are really only able to observe and discuss intelligent behavior and intelligent performance. From these observations, we extrapolate intelligence.

The study and identification of attributes of intelligence as reflected through intelligent behavior began in the nineteenth century. Herbert Spencer, who wrote *The Principles of Psychology* (1855), and Sir Francis Galton, whose work *Hereditary Genius* (1870) is a classic in the field, both believed in a general factor of intelligence related to but more important than other specific abilities. This theory was statistically confirmed by Charles Spearman, a pioneer in the statistical study of intelligence. Spearman's major works are *The Nature of Intelligence and the Principles of Cognition* (1923), and *Abilities of Man, Their Nature and Measurement* (1932). Spearman developed the statistical method of factor analysis, applied it to the results of intelligence tests, and concluded that there are two factors in intelligence, g and s. General ability or g, is pervasive in all kinds of tasks and is therefore most important. Specific, or s factors, are part of intelligent behaviors, but intelligence *per se* is characterized by a general way of behaving that equally affects all kinds of tasks.

The lack of agreement among researchers in the field is clearly seen by comparing Spearman's theory to that of another researcher, L.L. Thurstone, who, in *Multiple Factor Analysis: A Development and Expansion of the Vectors of Mind* (1924), identified seven basic abilities as being part of a "simple structure." These abilities were spatial, perceptual, numeric, verbal meaning, verbal fluency, memory, and inductive reasoning. He later identified an eighth, motor ability, in very young children. But he did not believe that there was an all-pervasive general factor involved.

Other researchers confirmed the existence of a general factor but found that it was not equally essential in the performance of all kinds of tasks. As a result, it has been proposed that there are intermediary group factors and also more specific abilities that relate and overlap in terms of application to the intelligent performance of tasks.

In addition, J. P. Guilford, in his classic work on the structure of the intellect, has proposed the existence of three large groups of abilities and 120 interrelating specific abilities. These are but a few of the researchers' theories about intelligence and its makeup. They summarize the major areas of both controversy and agreement among professionals in the field.

Although there is no consensus on a specific definition of intelligence, there are many areas of agreement about the general nature of intelligence. These are confirmed by the high correlation of the results from different intelligence tests.

IDEAL MODEL

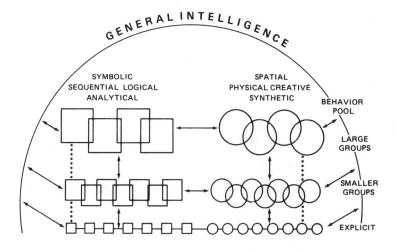

Interacting Structure of Intelligent Human Behaviors

First, there is a general intelligence ability that is used for various tasks and problems. This general ability or behavior is more critical in certain kinds of situations than in others. Further, there are secondary or group behaviors which are used in many situations, though they are not as pervasive as the general intelligence behavior. In addition, a larger set of smaller and more specific abilities comes into play in certain kinds of tasks. The general factor, large group behaviors, small group behaviors, and specific abilities overlap, interrelate, and interact. Most tasks with which a person is confronted tap more than one ability or behavior.

Whether behaviors are general, group, or specific, the behaviors and abilities referred to are mental or cognitive abilities. They relate to the functioning of the human brain. Intelligence tests are, in one sense, a method of measuring this mental capacity, and differences in I.Q. scores are indicative of differences in brain structure as well as differences that arise from exposure and experience.

Differences in Child and Adult Intelligence

Common sense and observation indicate that there are definite differences between the mental capabilities of children and those of adults. An average six-year-old, for example, cannot analyze and complete a problem in logic, cannot solve an algebraic equation, cannot read and comprehend Shakespeare—and no amount of "teaching" these will result in the child's mastery of them. Yet, many adults expect children to respond with the common sense and logic inherent in adult thinking. Such approaches to problem solving are quite outside the capabilities of the average child. This doesn't mean that children are illogical or that they have no common sense but that theirs is a logic and a common sense unique to the particular stage of development they are in at the specific time.

All humans develop physically and mentally in specific stages—each stage providing part of the foundation for adult-type thinking and each stage being incorporated into the next. The stages of development are characterized by methods used for acquiring information and the predominant modes of possible expression. Infants learn through exploration of the physical world by random movement, crawling, touching, and coming into direct physical contact with people and objects in the environment. They first learn essentially through activity controlled by the large muscles, and later by both large and small muscle activity.

During the period of time from birth to about two years of age, the child develops a foundation for future handling of language symbols, future control of self, and future socialization. The child touches, feels, and handles as many objects in the environment as possible. The child begins to acquire some of the skills for play and also begins to talk. Physical and mental development go hand in hand. If there is a deprivation of physical activity, mental foundations will go undeveloped. The child learns physically and expresses himself physically.

From about two to seven years of age, the child continues to learn through physical contact but also develops more refined ways of learning through the senses in coordination with large- and small-muscle activity. Around the time of three to four years of age, the child begins to play *with* other children—to cooperate and share. During this time the child develops at breakneck speed—in language and in social and mental activities. However, the child does not think like an adult, nor can the child express himself or herself through adult methods. There is a special kind of logic that parents often find exasperating. Wanting the "bigger" half is part of that logic. The child is unable to understand equalities as such and cannot possibly see or comprehend reverse relationships such as those needed for mathematical concepts. Another part of the typical four-year-old child's logic is the "magic rule" principle. If, for example, the child learns a rule of language, such as the past tense of "paint" is "painted," the _ed_ ending may be added to all words used in the past tense—runn_ed_, writ_ed_, and so on. Another example of this is found in the child's fascination with certain words or sounds that may be repeated over and over excessively. The "magic rule" principle is also extended into behavior of a slightly older age level in such children's games as "step on a crack and break your mother's back." A child of this age believes it to be a valid rule. Children at this stage of development have different rules for quantity than have adults. The child will prefer a tall glass of juice—it appears to hold more than a short glass—although an adult will easily recognize that the shorter glass is wider and actually contains the larger portion. This ability in *conservation* does not develop until sometime between the ages of seven and eleven years. How, then, can adults possibly expect a child to show the same type of logic and common sense as an adult when the child's normal physical–mental development prohibits such thinking?

Children at this stage also do not have an adult sense of time. They should be forming the beginning of such understandings as days of the week and ordinal relationships, but their time–

space concepts are quite undeveloped. They find it frustrating to wait for a reward, constantly asking, "How much longer?" The drawings of children at this age are also quite different from adult art. It is here that creativity is most often squelched when an adult insists that a picture "be" something or that it "look like a house or a tree," and so on. Children do not have a sense of perspective and will probably design pictures that show an "aerial" or "X-ray" view of the world. Space and size relationships will not be constant. The child's representations are extremely meaningful to the child and are also quite clear. They may be emotionally more accurate than a similar adult representation. For example, the child views the house as "home," with people and activity inside. Showing this kind of view is more sensitive and accurate from a functional point of view than the adult's concept of home or house in which the "walls" of secrecy cover up the life inside from the outside world. The child's art work is a mode through which he or she can express emotions and ideas which cannot yet be expressed in written and spoken language. It is also a basis for formal language and symbol development. As such, it needs to be accepted and encouraged as the child naturally develops from one level of expressional capability to the next.

Most children at the age of seven possess the attention skills and mental capabilities required for reading. They can mentally use a set of simple symbols by putting them together into meaningful wholes. They can learn to read. They cannot, however, read to learn until later. Similarly, they do not possess the methods or mental capabilities to learn by listening alone. Oral instruction needs to be combined with the use of other, more concrete, forms of physical and visual media for the learner at this stage to be able to assimilate and internalize the information intended. During this stage, the child develops the ability to understand reversibility, equivalents, and conservation, but the ability to perform formal abstract thinking and reasoning does not develop until somewhere between the ages of 11 and 15. The age at which a child acquires the mental capabilities of the next level of development is an indicator of intelligence. Highly intelligent children will be able to perform mental activi-

INTEGRATED LEARNING BEHAVIOR

LEARNS THROUGH
Conceptualizing,
seeing, touching

ABSTRACT-FORMAL
Abstract, conceptual,
mental development.
Systems of thinking and acting.
Adult reasoning and logic.

(+)

Seeing plus physical
contact

CONCEPTUAL-PERCEPTUAL
Information acquired
through senses and mentally
organized. Can act upon
environment.
Can group, compare,
analyze. Preformal thinking.

(+)

SENSORY-MOTOR
Small muscle, large muscle,
sensory exploration of real
world.
a. information more organized,
   more refined
b. basis for mental and social
   skills

(+)

Actual physical contact

PHYSICAL
Large muscles explore real world.
a. random movement
b. organized movement

Human Development and Mental Growth

ties and to reason in ways that are more mature than those of their less intelligent peers.

Once formal and abstract reasoning and thinking abilities have developed, the individual will have incorporated all the methods of learning from each of the developmental stages. Thus, he or she can learn through a variety and/or combination of physical, sensory, and conceptual modes. The individual can now address problems using the mental capabilities and methods of an adult.

The popular assumption is that general intelligence increases to about the age of 16 or 17 and then begins to decline. This assumption is based in part on the thesis that education enhances and promotes general intelligence. As intelligence is currently measured, this assumption is correct. However, there are many examples illustrating that general intelligence does not automatically decline during adulthood.

Much of the appearance of mental "slippage" may be attributed to specialization in job or profession. High levels of specialization cause the mental abilities that are not in daily use to lie fallow and become rusty from lack of exercise. The adult is not necessarily less intelligent, but his or her performance of intelligent behavior is more specialized and less generalized because some abilities are unused.

Adults who engage in less specialized activities or who continue education and general mental stimulation over a longer period of time, without limiting themselves in terms of interests will, as adults, achieve I.Q. scores within a reasonable range of those which they achieved as children. History is filled with examples of individuals who have been significantly productive and active in both academic and creative pursuits well into their later years. Although we do not have their I.Q. scores, such achievers as Grandma Moses, Winston Churchill, Pablo Picasso, Pablo Casals, Eleanor Roosevelt, Colonel Sanders, and Arthur Fiedler could not have continued to pursue activities requiring high performance and creativity in their senior years if their intelligence had significantly declined. They were intelligent, creative, lifelong learners and producers.

Brain Function: Creativity and Intelligence

In recent years research on the difference between left-brain and right-brain functions has cast new light on mental processing and on the relationship between intelligence and creativity. Traditionally, the left hemisphere of the brain has been referred to as the dominant hemisphere and the right hemisphere as the minor hemisphere. However, it is now believed that the dominance of one hemisphere over another is essentially the result of learning and mental exercise, not an inherent quality.

The difference between left- and right-brain functions is qualified by the mental activities which are processed in each half of the brain. The left hemisphere is the control center for such intellectual functions as memory, language, logic, computation, seriation, classification, writing, analysis, and convergent thinking. This encompasses the traditional skills and abilities necessary for academic success. It is the left-brain functions that are the primary skills of importance in tests of intelligence.

The right hemisphere is the control center for the mental functions involved in intuition, extrasensory perception, attitudes and emotions, visual and spatial relationships, music, rhythm, dance, physical coordination and activity, synthesis, and divergent thinking processes. Luthe (1976) characterizes left-brain thinking as "spotlight" thinking and right-brain thinking as "floodlight" thinking. This is a most picturesque, succinct, and accurate description of the difference between the two.

The functions of the left brain are characterized by sequence and order in comparison to the functions of the right brain, which are characterized as holistic and diffuse. The left brain can put the parts together into an organized whole; the right brain instinctively sees the whole, then the parts. Left-brain thinking is the essence of academic success and intelligence as it is currently measured; right-brain thinking is the essence of creativity. The two hemispheres must function in a balanced and integrated manner for wholesome human functioning to occur and for mental and physical health to be likewise in balance.

We live in a "left-brain" society, and nowhere is this more emphasized than in the schools. Schools are almost wholly oriented to the promotion and glorification of left-brain mental activity at the expense of the development of those activities which are right-brain functions. Thus, those individuals who are dominantly right-brain thinkers are out of tune to the drumbeat of most classroom and community settings. This is limiting not only to the youngsters who learn and express themselves through the creative, spatial, visual, physical, and holistic processes but also to the left-brain thinkers who have a large region of mental and physical functioning which goes undeveloped and unchallenged due to lack of exercise and practice.

Highly creative and highly intelligent individuals function with good balance in development and interaction between the two halves of the brain. In fact, creativity cannot occur in a vacuum; one must have information to draw upon from the left-brain abilities in order to act creatively.

This raises an intriguing possibility that the general factor of intelligence, which is so complex and difficult to define, may somehow be related to the integrated speed, efficiency, and flexibility of interaction between the left- and right-brain functions.

Following is a simple summary of some very complex information. It shows the principle of a general rule of brain activity. In actuality, it has been shown that there are small or minor areas in both hemispheres that are capable of carrying on the activities generally centered in the opposite half. For example, some language activity may be centered in the right brain; some visual–spatial activity may be centered in the left brain. In addition, the functions are generally reversed in a few individuals where the holistic type of thinking is controlled by the right hemisphere. This reversal of function seems more likely to be present in persons who are neither right- nor left-hand dominant—persons described as ambidextrous. On the whole, however, the general rule of differentiation of function applies.

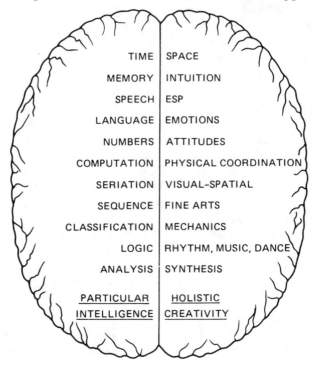

TIME	SPACE
MEMORY	INTUITION
SPEECH	ESP
LANGUAGE	EMOTIONS
NUMBERS	ATTITUDES
COMPUTATION	PHYSICAL COORDINATION
SERIATION	VISUAL-SPATIAL
SEQUENCE	FINE ARTS
CLASSIFICATION	MECHANICS
LOGIC	RHYTHM, MUSIC, DANCE
ANALYSIS	SYNTHESIS
PARTICULAR INTELLIGENCE	HOLISTIC CREATIVITY

Mental and Physical Health
INTELLIGENT CREATIVITY–CREATIVE INTELLIGENCE

Left-Brain, Right-Brain Mental Activities

A child who appears less intelligent than others on the basis of traditional tests and who has difficulty learning in a regular classroom may well be a visual–spatial, holistic learner rather than a slow learner. This is most likely to be true if the youngster shows evidence of good mental agility and capability when dealing with problems that require physical action or the manipulation of objects, rather than ideas, for a solution. Such a child may well be functionally handicapped in a schoolroom where instruction must be given which requires the child to use the dominant left-brain mental processes. Such a child will not only have difficulty with traditional instruction but will also experience frustration when the majority of learning is based solely on mastery of written and spoken language. This frustration will further add to the difficulty in learning as the child begins to view himself or herself as a person who cannot succeed. Continually lower scores on intelligence tests will accompany the frustration–failure syndrome and lack of learning experienced by the youngster.

The Significance of Right-Brain Intelligence to the Educational System and National Achievement

In the past several decades, the American educational system has moved from a state of deterioration to one of near catastrophe. As the nation approaches the twenty-first century and the ever-increasing complexity of modern society, the youth of the nation is ill-prepared to meet the challenges. A nation that fails to adequately educate its young virtually insures its own self-destruction. To understand the magnitude of our national educational failing, consider the following statistics:

1. The dropout rate in our high schools has reached a staggering 50% level! In an increasing number of major American cities, an even higher dropout rate is now being projected.

    Probably the most chilling aspect of this dropout situation is that over 50% of these dropouts are now estimated to be in the gifted and talented range! This means that many of the most creative minds in the nation are being lost to the system.

2. We are now annually graduating an estimated 750,000 high school students who are functionally illiterate. In a recent survey, a number of them could not even read their diplomas. With adult functional illiteracy already at the 20% level (1 out of 5), the total number is rapidly escalating and is adversely affecting the entire range of business and industry.

3. In a 1987 government study, high school graduates from the United States, Japan, Germany, and the

Soviet Union were tested for competency in mathematics and science. Of the students from Japan, Germany and the Soviet Union, 96% surpassed expected standards in both areas whereas only 6% from the United States exceeded those scores.

4. This growing population of dropouts, functional illiterates, and skill-deficient students is costing the nation an incredible *$84 billion dollars* annually in social services, drug-related crimes, and lost taxes. Moreover, the technological lead and status of the United States as a world leader is increasingly threatened by this deterioration of its educational system.

The key to ending the dropout problem lies in recognition of the special needs of right-brain dominated students. By far, the single largest factor in the increasing dropout rate in our educational system is the failure of the system to acknowledge and constructively address the difference between the way in which right-brain dominated people learn as opposed to the way in which left-brain dominated people learn.

First of all, our traditional education system is essentially a left-brain system. Information is given in a sequential, step-by-step process. In each subject area, we proceed in a linear fashion through a series of specifics. For left-brain dominated people, this is ideal since that is the way they process information.

Right-brain dominated people, however, do not learn well in this system because they do not process information in the same manner. They tend to interpret things holistically rather than in a sequence of details.

For example, in a mathematics class the teacher might present a problem on the board with a number of possible answers. A right-brain dominated student might quickly point to the correct answer. However, when asked by the teacher to explain the process by which he or she has arrived at the answer, the student cannot tell her. He or she just "knows" that is the answer. The student holistically grasps the problem and intuitively arrives at the answer, but cannot explain the process. The teacher may conclude that the answer is a lucky "guess" and advise the student that he or she must learn the process to pass the course.

Right-brain dominated people tend to grasp the total concept—and then go back and dissect the information into its component parts. This processing is the *reverse* of the traditional approach to learning. Right-brain people are visually oriented: pictures, diagrams, etc., enhance their learning. They also absorb much information aurally (by ear). In a learning situation (class), right-brain dominated persons *must* be allowed to explore and discuss their "hunches" and their Gestaltist insights and to ask wide-ranging questions that their holistic view of most situtations quickly generates. To dismiss their questions as irrelevant and to deny them the opportunity for open discusssion is to severely retard their learning and to virtually insure their failure in an academic setting. They are often extremely intelligent and creative people but have difficulty in conforming to a left-brain learning system. It is like trying to fit a round peg into a square hole. Because such students do not analyze information or respond in the expected sequential manner, they are often perceived to be "slow learners" and are shunted aside. The negative self-image developed by these students is often devastating. The conviction that they cannot learn becomes a self-fulfilling prophecy for many of them. In compensation for their "failure," some become disruptive and troublesome while many, convinced of the absurdity and futility of the sytem, simply "opt out" or quit altogether.

These right-brain dominated "failures" are assumed to constitute the majority of our high-school and college dropouts.

The origins of our present left-brain educational system are deeply rooted in the historical development of Western culture.

In earlier, more primitive societies, the right-brain skills so necessary to survival played a far more prominent role in the culture. The intuition and creative adaptation of right-brain thinking to the vagaries of nature and unexpected calamities was far more fundamental to existence than it is in our current, more orderly left-brain society.

The Renaissance, with its emphasis upon science, mathematics, and logical reasoning, led to the Industrial Revolution which, in turn, produced a sweeping change in Western culture. The right-brain skills so prized and predominant in our earlier society were quickly forced into the background and were superseded by an emphasis upon facts, logic, and structure—the special province of left-brain thinking. Today, in our twentieth century factory, office, and business establishments, there is an overwhelming preponderance of left-brain thinking and the rewards of the society go to those who conform to its dictates. With the rising affluence created by this more materially productive and orderly society, virtually all of our modern social, business, and government institutions have been structured into rigid, left-brain hierarchies of thinking and performance. Max Weber's monumental study of bureaucracy magnificently details this awesome left-brain conversion of our Western society into its existing form.

Nowhere in our society, however, has the left-brain cognitive mode been more rigidly imposed than in our educational system. The unyielding insistence—often by well-intentioned teachers, administrators, and parents—of complete conformity to a left-brain system of learning and performance is rapidly depleting one of our nation's greatest resources—our creative right-brain dominated youth. The rising tide of mediocrity of performance among our young people closely parallels the suppression of right-brain thinking in our schools. And these are the nation's potential leaders and creative problem solvers.

Approximately 38% of the American people are estimated to be right-brain dominated, and the failure of our traditional educational system to recognize this reality and to adjust the teaching methodology to accomodate this population is now producing a national disaster.

Methodology for Teaching Right-Brain Dominated People

To maximize learning, right-brain dominated people must be taken through all three phases of learning: input, assimilation, and output. The diagram below illustrates these three essential phases of learning.

PHASE I	PHASE II	PHASE III
INPUT	**ASSIMILATION**	**OUTPUT**

LISTENING

SEEING

READING

HUMAN MIND

SPEAKING

WRITING

NONVERBAL ACTIONS

To obtain maximum retention of knowledge, the individual *must* go through *all three* phases—regardless of whether the objective is the learning of Latin, of mechanics, or of any other subject.

If the individual goes through only the first two phases, the knowledge retention level is approximately 20%. This, basically, is the situation in our traditional educational system. The student sitting in class reads, listens, and observes but rarely proceeds to the third learning phase by interacting with the teacher or with other students.

In contrast, where the student is involved *in all three phases* of learning—input, assimilation, and output through discussion, writing, etc.—the retention level rises dramatically to a *90% level*. Learning is accelerated and students learn *much more* in a *much shorter time*.

Of special significance in this three-phase learning approach is that in the third (output) phase it affords the right-brain dominated student the opportunity for vitally needed discussion.

In our traditional educational system with its large class size (30 to 35 students), such a three-phase methodology is difficult to implement. No matter how gifted or dedicated the teacher, it is impossible to deal effectively with 30 to 35 individual learning rates. Moreover, given the physical time restraints, the teacher cannot effectively involve each student in the vital output phase of the learning. As long as this situation continues, we shall continue to witness a growing dropout rate and a deterioration of national educational performance.

To correct the situation, we must restructure the educational system dramatically. Classes must be made much smaller. Fewer subjects should be taught at one time, and the classes must be student-centered, with each student actively involved in the third learning phase, i.e., discussion, questions and answers, etc. Not only will such methodology reduce the dropout of our right-brain dominated students, but it will also greatly accelerate the learning rate of the left-brain dominated students.

Contrary to popular opinion, such methodology does *not* require more teachers or increased educational cost. Because the student learns more quickly and more completely in such a system, much less class time is required to achieve high levels of knowledge acquisition. Such methodology could quickly be implemented throughout our educational system with the necessity neither for higher expenditures nor for more teachers.

Such a restructuring would bring enormous benefit to the students and would be a boon to the teachers—for whom such an approach is the near ideal in teaching. Yet, there is little likelihood that such will be implemented at any time in the foreseeable future in the traditional system. However, we should like to present a model for the future, Hawthorne University's

"2 + 2" Academy Program, which has created a dynamically effective model for such a methodology.

In 1986, Hawthorne University in Salt Lake City, through its Academy Division, implemented its highly successful "2 + 2" program. High school students who had finished the sophomore or 10th grade of high school were allowed to enroll in a combined, high school/college two-year curriculum, based upon the above-described three-phased approach to learning. In the two-year program, students completed not only high school, but a two-year college degree as well.

Following a regular collegiate schedule, students were placed in small classes of 10 to 12 students each, and were seated around conference tables in graduate-type seminars. Each class was an intensive, Socratic discussion of the material under study, and each student was intimately involved in the process. For each hour of class, there was an outside study requirement of two to three hours. Students carried only two subjects each term, but the coverage was intensive and the course was completed in that term. Over the three academic terms of the year, six specific subjects were completed. All instruction was college level. At the end of each course, students took national college proficiency examinations such as CLEP (College Level Examination Program), AP (Advanced Placement), etc.

The results of the program were startling and dramatic.

The methodology not only involved the students in all three phases of learning, but it also addressed the needs of the right-brain dominated students. There was a tremendous increase in motivation and a precipitous rise in the learning rate in every subject taken.

Fully 80% of the students enrolled initially in the program were right-brain dominated and were either dropouts or "at risk" students. Many previously had been C, D, or F grade students in their high schools. To show just how dramatic was the turnaround, the following is a mean-score summary of these initial twenty-one high school juniors enrolled in the Hawthorne program on the national college proficiency examinations (CLEP) after the first six months:

Score Scale	Western Civilization-I 20–80	College Composition 20–80	Humanities 200–800
Pretest score	29	31	270
National Percentile Rank	1	4	1
Final Test Score	57	51	547
National Percentile Rank	75	53	84
Percentage of Increase in Test Scores	97	65	103
Increase in National Percentile Rank	74 times	13 times	83 times

The rise in scores after just six months of instruction was far beyond what might have been expected of these previously mediocre students.

Today, these right-brain dominated high school students in the Hawthorne Academy program are literally setting national achievement records. Not only are many of them scoring in the upper 50th percentile in the college proficiency examinations, but 95% are completing the program with 3–4.0 grade point averages. On the national college entrance examinations (ACT and SAT) the scores of these Hawthorne students are just as dramatic. For example, the national ACT average for high school seniors is 18 (out of a possible 36). The lowest score for a Hawthorne student to date is 21 and the average is 25, fully seven points above the national average!

These results at Hawthorne University hold significant implications for our educational system and provide one of the answers to reversing the catastrophic dropout of our right-brain dominated young people and the deterioration of our educational system. The five-year-old program proves conclusively that we can "rescue" our talented and creative right-brain dominated students by the use of such innovative and motivating educational methodology in our schools.

I.Q. Test Analysis: Left-Brain, Right-Brain Abilities

Now that you have been introduced to the concept of right-brain and left-brain, you are probably very curious about where you fit in. The I.Q. test you took at the beginning of the book taps both left-brain and right-brain abilities.

You may have done extremely well on one type of question, but not so well on the other. Most people will find one type of question easier, but will have abilities in both areas. As noted in an earlier section of this book, it is not possible to construct a paper and pencil test which comprehensively tests the right-brain types of abilities. However, while most paper and pencil I.Q. tests are essentially tests of left-brain functions, each specific item in the test can be analyzed for its left-brain, right-brain components, and from this analysis some very interesting conclusions may be drawn.

We have carefully analyzed each specific question on your I.Q. test and have placed each into one of two categories. The first category contains those questions that test predominantly left-brain functions; the second category contains those questions that test both left- and right-brain functions. By identifying those questions which required right-brain processing on your part, you may gain further insight into your own I.Q. score.

Return now to your I.Q. test and, on the analysis sheet on page 62, list under Category I the left-brain questions that you missed and under Category II the right-brain questions that you got wrong. Then carefully review *all* the questions from *both* categories that you had *correct* and in the last column list those questions from among your correct answers that were "just right guesses." By comparing these three columns, we can come to a number of conclusions:

1.   If you missed a fairly equal number of items from both those itemized as left-brain and those characterized as right-brain, then the possibility is that there is a dominance of neither right- nor left-brain processing. In other words, you employ a balanced left- and right-brain processing in most problems and questions that you encounter.

2.   If most of the questions that you missed fall into the second category (questions requiring right-brain processing), then the probability is that you are a left-brain oriented individual who tends to approach and answer problems and questions primarily through left-brain processing.

3.   If most of the questions that you missed are under the left-brain category, it may indicate that you are primarily or dominantly a right-brain thinker. If you did quite well on the questions which are based on or require right-brain skills but did not score particularly high on the test, you may very well be a very intelligent right-brain thinker. An in-depth individual test which is professionally administered and which includes the "performance" type of questions and problems would give you a better analysis of your abilities and of your I.Q.

4.   Take another look at the number of questions at which you guessed but which you answered correctly. These answers were arrived at through intuitive thinking, which is a *right-brain* process. It is most likely, especially if there are several of these, that they were not wild guesses but were arrived at through the right-brain intuitive function's interacting at an unconscious level with information stored deep in the left-brain memory bank. These answers, regardless of the category of the questions, are indicative of right-brain functioning.

Category I: Left-Brain Questions

1. Primarily a left-brain question that taps abilities in sequencing and analysis. It also requires the right-brain ability to recognize position in space.

2. A left-brain question tapping abilities in classification, analysis, general information, and memory.

5. A left-brain question requiring mathematical and sequencing skills.

6. A left-brain question tapping classification, memory, analysis, and general informational abilities.

7. This is a left-brain question requiring information, memory, analysis, and general informational abilities.

8. A left-brain question tapping classification, memory, information, and analysis skills.

10. A left-brain question tapping ability in logic and analysis.

11. A left-brain question requiring mathematical, informational, and memory skills.

13. A left-brain question requiring logic and analysis.

16. A left-brain question requiring numerical, mathematical, informational, memory, and analysis skills.

17. A left-brain question tapping classification, information, and memory.

18. A left-brain question requiring language and analysis skills.

20. A left-brain question tapping mathematical, informational, memory, and analysis skills.

*22. A left-brain question requiring language, information, and memory. However, if you arrived at the answer through a mental picture of the garden where these vegetables grow, you are relying on right-brain processing in problem solving.

23. A left-brain question tapping classification, information, memory, analysis, and analogy.

24. A left-brain question requiring numerical and mathematical skills, information, and memory.

*26. A left-brain question in logic and analysis. However, if you arrived at an answer by using a pictorial diagram, you are relying to a great extent on right-brain information processing.

28. A left-brain question requiring mathematical and analysis skills along with memory and general information.

29. A left-brain question tapping language, general information, memory, and classification.

30. A left-brain question tapping information, memory, analysis, and classification skills.

32. A left-brain question tapping mathematical, informational, memory, sequencing, and analysis skills.

33. A left-brain question requiring language, information, classification, analysis, and memory skills.

34. A left-brain question requiring language, information, memory, classification, and analysis.

35. A left-brain question tapping language, classification, and analysis skills.

36. A left-brain question tapping mathematical, informational, memory, and analysis skills.

38. A left-brain question tapping language, sequencing, informational, memory, and classification skills. The right-brain position-in-space function is also related.

39. A left-brain question requiring mathematical, memory, and informational and analysis skills.

41. A left-brain question requiring language, classification, and analysis skills.

43. A left-brain question requiring language, information, sequencing, and analysis skills. The right-brain function of position-in-space also comes into play.

44. A left-brain skill requiring mathematical, informational, memory, sequencing, and analysis skills.

45. A left-brain question tapping information, memory, classification, and analysis abilities.

48. A left-brain question requiring logic and analysis skills.

50. A left-brain question tapping language, memory, and analysis abilities.
52. A left-brain question requiring language, information, memory, classification, and analysis skills.
53. A left-brain question tapping language, information, memory, classification, and analysis skills.
55. A left-brain question tapping mathematical, informational, memory, and analysis skills.
56. A left-brain question tapping logic and analysis skills.
58. A left-brain question tapping language, information, classification, memory, and analysis abilities.
60. A left-brain question tapping language, classification, information, memory, and analysis abilities.

Category II: Right-Brain Questions

3. A right-brain question based on ability to see relationships in space and form. It also requires left-brain skills in classification.
4. This question taps both the right-brain skills in space and form and left-brain number skills.
9. A right-brain question requiring ability in space and form, but also requiring left-brain skills in classification and analogy.
12. A right-brain question tapping abilities in space and form, but also requiring left-brain skills in classification and analysis.
14. A right-brain question tapping abilities in space–form relationships, but also requiring left-brain skills in classification and analysis.
15. A question tapping the right-brain abilities in spatial relationships but also requiring left-brain analysis and sequencing.
19. A question that is right-brain in terms of the information with which it deals but left-brain in that it taps abilities in vocabulary, analogy, and analysis.

21. A right-brain question dealing with space and form relationships, but also requiring left-brain abilities of analysis and analogy.

*22. A left-brain question requiring language, information, and memory. However, if you arrived at the answer through a mental picture of the garden where these vegetables grow, you are relying on right-brain processing in problem solving.

25. A right-brain question tapping abilities in space–form relationships which also requires left-brain skills of classification and analysis.

*26. A left-brain question in logic and analysis. However, if you arrived at an answer by using a pictorial diagram, you are relying to a great extent on right-brain information processing.

27. A right-brain question tapping space and form relationships, but also requiring left-brain numerical skills.

31. A right-brain question tapping informational, memory, analysis, and classification skills.

37. A right-brain question tapping abilities in space–form relationships and requiring left-brain classification and analysis.

40. A right-brain question tapping space–form relationship abilities and requiring left-brain skills in classification and analysis.

42. A combination of right- and left-brain skills. The question is based on ability to gain information through visual images but requires the left-brain functions of information, memory, classification, and analysis.

46. A right-brain question requiring abilities in space–form relationships, but also requiring left-brain skills in numbers.

47. A right-brain question requiring abilities in spatial relationships, but also requiring left-brain number skills.

49. A right-brain question requiring abilities in space and form relationships, but also tapping left-brain numerical skills and abilities in classification and analysis.

51. A right-brain question tapping space–form relationship skills, but also requiring left-brain abilities in classification, numbers, and analysis.

54. A question based on ability to process right-brain visual-image information but requiring left-brain information, classification, and analysis skills.

57. A question that taps right-brain position-in-space abilities but which is heavily left-brain in requiring language, information, memory, sequencing, and analysis skills.

59. A question that deals with right-brain position-in-space skills but which also requires left-brain language, sequencing, and information and analysis skills.

The foregoing analysis of left- and right-brain functioning is based upon several factors:

1. The questions on the I.Q. test that tap right-brain functions also require abilities which are essentially left-brain. However, *the reverse* is *not true*. Most left-brain questions on the test which deal with language and numbers do not necessarily require right-brain abilities.

   We are thus able to identify and separate the questions into two different categories.

2. Right-brain thinkers, when confronted with questions of language, logic, or mathematics—which are essentially left-brain problems—may use pictures or diagrams or may think in mental pictures in an effort to solve them. Or they "guess"—which is an intuitive, right-brain response.

   In brief, they are applying right-brain processing to left-brain questions. Thus, the list of correct "guesses" on the test is a further strong indication of right-brain functioning.

Although the analysis is far from precise, it will give you a good indication of whether you employ balanced or predominantly left- or right-brain processing in your approach to the problems confronting you in your everyday life.

Such insight might well be significant. If, for example, the indication is that you are predominantly left-brain oriented, perhaps you are overlooking or neglecting the development of some creative or artistic talent which you may possess.

If the indications are that you are predominantly right-brain oriented, then you are essentially a creative individual who tends to think holistically or in patterns and who may, therefore, have encountered past difficulties in a left-brain-oriented society.

Left-Brain, Right-Brain
Test Analysis

CATEGORY I: LEFT-BRAIN	CATEGORY II: RIGHT-BRAIN	GUESSES

Creativity

Although the intelligence required for traditional academic success is generally the result of mental activity peculiar to left-brain processing, the creativity of open and original production is the result of mental activity peculiar to right-brain processing. The first is sequentially ordered, analytical, logical, and temporal; the second is intuitive, diffuse, and spatial. The left-brain process allows the carefully ordered building of a whole from its many parts. The right-brain process allows an almost intuitive grasping of the whole in relationship to its parts.

Creativity was once thought of as a process or activity that was unique to production and performance in art, music, and drama. Creative production and performance exist, however, in all areas of human endeavor. These include not only the visual and performing arts, but also the academic disciplines, the professions, government and politics, and so on. The creative producer or performer is one who brings innovation and new lifeforms into any field of human activity: the scientist who discovers a new vaccine; the coach who invents a new offensive tactic; the businessperson who creates a new and needed service; the researcher who develops a new theory about human behavior—all such activities and more are examples of creative endeavor in areas outside the visual and performing arts.

Creativity requires individuality, independence of thought and action, spontaneity, originality, and flexibility of action combined with dedication to purpose. It is more than spontaneous, original, flexible, and independent thought, however. Although this type of thinking is essential and can occur only where there is a free and unencumbered flow of ideas, images, and emotions, such ideas and thoughts cease to be spontaneous and original after a period of time elapses subsequent to their emergence. In addition to creative thinking, creativity involves a sense of purpose coupled with action. The creative act requires that emerging ideas and thoughts be organized into new or different patterns from their previous organization. The creative act has a result—a product, material, service, or mental structure. This result, in order to meet the criteria of creativity, must be different from similar previous structures.

All humans possess the ability to create or to be creative. For many persons this innate creative ability is squelched before they even enter school, or, if not by that time, then shortly thereafter. This is because of the cultural–social emphasis upon conformity, acceptance, doing the "right" thing, finding the "correct" answer. Some creative ability can be recaptured later on, even in adulthood, but once the individual has learned to suppress the basic and necessary mental and personality activities of the creative process, the chances are slim for later development of full potential.

All human beings possess creative ability, but not all possess the creative talent of a Beethoven, Picasso, Einstein, or Edison. There is a difference between ordinary and super creativity. This difference is not really a difference in the process; rather, it represents different points on a continuum of ability or talent. For example:

Continuum of Creativity

There are tests available for the measurement of creativity, but the results that are generated are not mathematically specific as they are with intelligence tests. Levels of creative talent cannot be broken down into specific levels of performance or potential but might be viewed as a surging and churning ocean current whose visible peaks are manifest in the ebb and flow of magnificent, unrestricted waves breaking in toward a distant and undefined shore.

Tests of creativity provide questions and problems for which there are no "best" or "right" answers. Their purpose is the testing of divergent thinking styles. Among the types of questions used on such tests are the following.

1. **The Untitled Story:** a short, one-paragraph story is presented and the individual is asked to suggest titles for it. The question is scored on the basis of: a) quantity—the number of titles offered; and b) quality—the originality or uniqueness of the title suggestions. For example:

Write newspaper headlines for this story:

> Jake Rush, a local private eye, was found today crushed by a grease pit hoist in an abandoned Pittman Street garage. Jake's body was found stuffed in a large plastic bag. Jake had apparently been attempting to escape since he had poked a hole in the bag. Clutched in his hand were the dusty remnants of the jewels recently stolen from the internationally reknowned Groist Ltd. diamond firm. Mr. Rush had been hired by the insurance agency of Crouch, Inc., to assist in the investigation and recovery of the stolen jewels. Detectives theorized that Rush tried to singlehandedly apprehend the criminals in their hideaway and was overpowered from behind. The jewels had apparently been stashed in a hole at the bottom of the pit, and Rush found them just before his untimely end. There is a question as to whether Rush's estate will receive the recovery reward.

Examples of Ordinary Titles: "Private Eye Found Dead"; "Detective Crushed by Hoist"; "Jake Rush Killed by Thieves"

Examples of Creative Titles: "Rush Crushed"; "Ouch-Pouch End for Crouch P.I."; "Groist Wiped Out by Hoist"; "Drastic Plastic Reward"

2. **The Untitled Cartoon or Caricature:** scored in the same way as the untitled story.

Ordinary Captions: "Help!" "Don't just stand there!"

Creative Captions: "Give my regards to Broadway!" "Quick! Call 855-3267 and ask if John Smith's life insurance premium has been paid!"

3. **Paired Words:** Pairs of words which appear to have no relationship to each other are presented. The individual is asked to name a third word which is somehow related or common to the other two. For example:

sugar: walking   (*cane*)
bank: story   (*teller*)
eye: meow   (*cat's*)
day: pipe   (*dream*)

This type of question has obvious limitations. Suggested answers are available. If the scorer is not creative enough to recognize the validity of unnamed possibilities, it fails as a test of creativity and becomes a test of convergent thinking ability.

4. **Visual Fill-In:** Partly completed pictures or designs are presented. The individual might be asked to give as many interpretations as possible of what the design might represent, be, or become. For example:

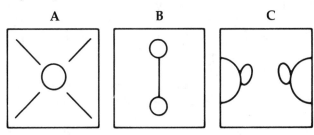

This question is scored on the basis of quantity and uniqueness of answers.

Examples of Ordinary Answers: A. sun; B. barbell; C. two cup handles

Examples of Creative Answers: A. four-legged spider; inside of a well; spaceship, front or rear view; intersection with round, fat crossing guard; B. door handle; two knotholes hooked together by crack; stereo headset; two floating balloons; part of a necklace; old-fashioned telephone earpiece; C. two clowns whispering; two rabbits going in opposite directions; mirror image of left ear; mirror image of right ear; ludicrous freeway loops

Note that the creative answers are more than unique and original; they exhibit richness and fluency of both thought and language.

5. **Object Uses:** Subject is given an example of an ordinary object and asked to name as many different uses for the object as possible. For example, the object might be a pencil. The common answer would be to

use for writing or drawing. Creative answers would include such things as: houseplant stake; back-scratcher; stringholder, and so on.

These are a few examples of the types of questions used in tests of creativity. Some of the limitations of such tests are obvious. First is the time required for scoring, which is extensive. Second, the creativity of the test designer will place both upper and lower limits on the levels of creativity taken into account. Third, the creativity of the test scorer is critical. The scorer must be able to recognize the validity of relationships and possibilities which are not offered in the suggested guidelines for scoring.

There is a more simple and effective method for determining the possibilities for creativity of an individual: the observation of the person's behavior over a period of time. One must first identify some of the behaviors that indicate creative potential and performance. Among these are a prolific quantity of ideas along with uniqueness of ideas. Other behaviors include: independence and individuality in thought and action; curiosity; originality; self-assertiveness; fluency; process (rather than product) orientation; sensitivity to beauty; sensitivity to emotions (one's own and those of others); self-honesty; willingness to take risks; willingness to be different; self-motivation; unusual and active imagination; ability to live with uncertainty; adaptability and flexibility; intuition; persistence; production of innovative ideas and things; a keen and sometimes unusual sense of humor.

Logical thinking and analysis can be performed on schedule. Creativity cannot. In the creative process there is first a period of readiness or openness. This may involve the acquisition of information and ideas, studying or identifying a problem, and constructing some sort of hypothesis. Readiness is followed by a sort of incubation period in which the individual mulls over, lives with, and thinks about possibilities for new organization. Sometimes during incubation, insight occurs. Insight may come after a few hours or days, or it might take months or even years. This is the part of the creative process that cannot be forced. It is depicted in cartoons as a light bulb's being suddenly turned on inside a person's head, and this is probably the most succinct and vivid description of what happens when all the possibilities have been synthesized into a new organization or problem solution. After that, it is a matter of producing the actual result and then perhaps testing it out to see if it works as imagined.

Creativity and the creative process cannot be rushed, and there are no magic limits on the various stages. A stage might take minutes or years. Creative people are noted, however, for persistence. They will persist toward a goal with great flexibility but also with commitment. It is this persistence that represents the significant difference between the productively creative individual and the simple original thinker or idea generator.

Intelligence and intelligent capabilities are necessary for creativity to result in "good" products. The creative mind must have information, ideas, and concepts from which to draw. Although highly creative people do not necessarily *show* high I.Q. scores, they would not be capable of creative endeavor as described here if their intelligence capabilities were extremely low. When reference is made to "highly intelligent, highly creative" persons, the reference is to individuals who are highly creative and who have actual, though unregistered, I.Q.s of 140 to 150 or even above. Experience shows that a majority of unusually creative persons tend to score between 120 and 139 on standard intelligence tests. Whether such persons are more creative than intelligent or whether they score lower on convergent types of intelligence tests because they are divergent types of thinkers is a question that cannot be answered.

Are Intelligence Scores Useful and Important?

For a long time there has been a great deal of controversy among educators and parents over the use of intelligence scores and their validity. Too often, children have been incorrectly labeled as having less ability and/or potential than they actually possess, and they have been placed in very limiting educational settings as a result. It is not only the placement that is a tragedy in such a case; it is the predictive factor of future success and basic underlying attitudes toward self that are extremely destructive. Unfortunately, it is true that human beings tend to fulfill the prophecies made on their behalf.

The controversy, however, is not over the use of intelligence tests but over their *misuse*. Any long-term decisions about a child's educational needs or placement in the educational setting should take into consideration a series of I.Q. scores along with a host of other behaviors that are not and cannot be identified through such tests.

A low score on an intelligence test may signal that a child needs different methods of instruction. A learning-disabled child, for example, who does not receive early and sound remedial assistance and concrete forms of instruction in school will very likely show a test pattern of decreasing test scores between entering school and arriving at about a sixth-grade or 12- or 13-year-old level. The child may be quite intelligent, but because of poor language and math skills he or she will increasingly appear to learn like a slow learner and test like a slow learner. Recent trends toward mainstreaming all children should be helpful in reducing such educational travesties, particularly when different kinds of instruction and instructional media are made available to learners whose needs are different from those of the other students.

Another swirl of controversy over the use of intelligence tests revolves around the possibility of "cultural bias." Cultural bias refers to the possibility that a test may be appropriate only for individuals whose backgrounds have prized, promoted, and/or taught certain skills. For example, traditional intelligence tests assumed thinking skills and language skills that a person would acquire from an average, English-speaking middle-class background. A person for whom English was a second language and/or whose cultural environment stressed different values would be laboring under a handicap in trying to answer the traditional questions that were asked. Most tests today have been rewritten in attempts to eliminate such bias. An important point to emphasize here is that even though a test may indeed be culturally biased and therefore not give the best indication of "intelligence," the results from intelligence tests are generally quite accurate in predicting future success in the school situation as schools are presently structured. This leads to the next point—that along with further research and effort to develop truly culture-free tests the real problem may need to be addressed within the structure of the schools.

In spite of the controversy over intelligence tests, it has been shown that the results give a good indication not only of a child's probable future success in school but also of future success as an adult. The classic long-term study of about 1500 highly intelligent schoolchildren which was begun in 1921 by Lewis M. Terman, and published in 1926 and later as the *Genetic Studies of Genius* series, has resulted in some very significant and interesting information along this line. This study has observed the individuals identified in 1921 as highly intelligent over a period of many years and at different checkpoints throughout their adulthood. Although the study will not be complete until after the year 2000, the results to date show that these individuals have achieved significant rewards and recognition, have an unusually high degree of success professionally and financially, enjoy better health and longer lifespans than their less gifted contemporaries, with few exceptions. All in all, the highly intelligent have proved by behavior and performance to be outstanding in achievement, educational levels, contributions to society, career success, and health compared to others less gifted.

The final philosophical area of controversy over intelligence tests rests on the conviction of many people that it is inappropriate to try to specifically measure something that cannot be specifically defined. Indeed, the concept of intelligence is a very complex and abstract idea over which even professionals do not fully share a consensus of opinion in the matter of definition. Alfred Binet, the "father" of intelligence tests and the author of the 1905 *Binet Intelligence Scale,* was a Paris psychologist of the late nineteenth and early twentieth centuries who was given the task of finding a way to identify children in the Paris schools who were not capable of handling regular schoolwork and of learning in a traditional classroom setting. In an attempt to identify such handicapped learners, Binet began identifying the skills and abilities that were necessary for children of different ages to succeed in school. He then developed a test based upon samples of questions and problems that children who can learn successfully should be able to complete. This was the first I.Q. test, and its purpose was to identify handicapped learners. When Binet was asked, however, what intelligence is, he replied by saying that it is what his test measures. This may seem like a ludicrous definition, but it is actually the key to a basis for defining intelligence—a way of performing or behaving.

Not only did Binet define intelligence as what his test measured, but he further suggested that it was more fruitful to set about the task of measuring and studying it than to engage in academic arguments relative to its definition. Other prominent researchers have attempted both, and a look at some of their definitions will provide some insight into our definition of intelligence.

Terman described it as "the ability to carry on abstract thinking"; Woodrow, another of the early analyzers of intelligence, as "the capacity to acquire capacity"; Thurstone, in his 1924 *The Nature of Intelligence,* as "the capacity to live a trial-and-error existence with alternatives which are not yet complete." (This alludes to aspects of creative behavior.) Wechsler, developer of the "Wechsler Intelligence Scale" and author of *Measurement and Appraisal of Adult Intelligence* (1972), defined it as "the aggregate or global capacity to act purposefully, to think rationally, and to deal effectively with [the] environment."

Other definitions imply speed, efficiency, and innate ability or potential. All of these are partly correct. Intelligence, as described here, is reflected in *human* behavior. While some animals may be taught specific abilities, such as "fetching" or "prancing" or "balancing a ball" or finding the way through a maze, few if any animals would "score" well on a general intelligence test. Intelligence, in a sense, separates humans from other forms of animal life. Some humans have more intelligence than others. Some have different kinds of intelligence. However, intelligence in general is characterized by *a mental process that incorporates speed, efficiency, agility, and flexibility in the purposeful mental activity of dealing with life tasks, problem solving, and the production of both conventional and innovative ideas, services, and products. It requires not only the ability to apply attained skills but also the ability to acquire new ones.*

Intelligence tests, although accurate in the type of predictions that they can support, do have limitations. They measure intelligence only as defined by convergent, as compared to divergent, ways of thinking. Convergent thinking is the kind of mental process used to arrive at answers which are predetermined—the best or right answer in a given set of circumstances. This kind of thinking and approach to problem solving is the one predominantly fostered in schools and the one prized in many families. It is the kind of thought process used to answer conventional multiple-choice or true–false types of questions; it is the type of thought process used to determine the types of values to be applied when concerning oneself about "what other people will think." It is closed and not very dynamic, although in logical and analytical applications it can pose high challenges. It is the type of thinking that largely comprises measured intelligence.

Divergent thought, on the other hand, is characterized by openness and the production of unique and original answers and solutions. It is the thought process associated with creativity, individuality, and difference. While prized in some families and in a few educational settings, it goes relatively unreinforced and unnurtured in our society.

The inability of intelligence tests to measure or require the application of divergent thinking behavior—along with schooling's emphasis upon convergent types of thinking and abstract, verbal, and sequential methods of presenting learning material—often stands in the way of identifying intelligence and giftedness in individuals who are not convergent types of thinkers. History confirms the misinterpretation and misunderstanding of the abilities of certain individuals who have proven to be highly gifted and talented and even of genius stature as adults.

For example, Hermann von Helmholtz, whose contributions in the fields of physics and mathematics were gigantic in nature, did not do well or impress his teachers while a student. Although extremely talented in mathematics, other school tasks of a routine and convergent nature did not allow him the independence of thought necessary for creative endeavor. He spent his time daydreaming, thinking through ideas of interest to him, and paying little attention to required schoolwork.

Noted poet Ralph Waldo Emerson graduated in the bottom half of his class. Thomas Edison was told that he was too stupid to learn. Albert Einstein did not talk until he was three years old and learned to read much later than most children. He did very poorly in school. John B. Watson, noted psychologist, was described by teachers as lazy and insubordinate. Eleanor Roosevelt was viewed by teachers as having few redeeming qualities. She was looked upon as a withdrawn daydreamer who came out of her shell only during selfish attempts to be the center of attention. Ludwig von Beethoven's music teacher considered him a washout as a composer. Jan Masaryck, while visiting the United States as a child, was labeled retarded on the basis of one I.Q. test and was briefly institutionalized as a result.

These are but a few examples of the inappropriate evaluations of highly intelligent, creative, and divergent thinkers who were believed to have little or no ability because they were *different*. All can be identified as basically creative, individualistic, highly intelligent persons who did not fit into the classical convergent structure of the schools.

Such individuals as those noted above may be misevaluated for a number of reasons. They may be so highly intelligent that routine classroom learning is boring and dull. In their refusal to participate, they turn to daydreaming and/or unacceptable classroom behavior. They may also be highly creative instead of, or in addition to, being highly intelligent. Their thinking processes may not fit into traditional educational settings. They may often be infinitely more intelligent and/or creative than their teachers, who have little understanding of and empathy for their needs. They may have learning difficulties that interfere with their ability to learn in abstract and conventional ways. Or, the misevaluated student may be subjected to a test which is completely inappropriate because of language and cultural differences.

In any event, such children may be daydreamers, wisecrackers, or have other types of behavior problems. There are other reasons for youngsters to behave in ways that are not very acceptable to teachers, but the possibility of high intelligence and high creativity should never be overlooked.

Can Intelligence Be Improved or Raised?

Whether or not intelligence can be raised rests on whether general intelligence is inherited or learned. Which is the more important factor—heredity or environment? This has been a subject of controversy for many years.

Traditionally, it was believed that intelligence was an inherited ability, as there seemed to be evidence of high intelligence and achievement in certain families. However, with the growth and impact of knowledge accumulated in the behavioral and social sciences came an interest and belief in the importance of environment with respect to individual abilities and achievements. Volumes of research exist in support of both ideas, and controversy still surrounds the issue.

Common sense, however, dictates the importance and impact of both heredity and environment on both intelligence and achievement. Since the complexity of brain structure is related to intelligent behavior, obviously heredity is a factor. Think of brain structure and the complexity of neural connections as analogous to a network. It follows that the brain structure and capacity linked with high intelligence are like a highly developed urban network of freeways and their interchanges, while the brain structure of low intelligence is akin to a rural dirt crossroads. There is, then, some kind of innate potential which is inherited and which is related to the structure of the brain—the complexity of connections and its processing capabilities. In this sense, the upper limits of a person's intelligence are predetermined before birth. However, other factors—both physiological and environmental—do affect the development of intelligent capacity and intelligent capability.

First, the average person uses less than 15% to 20% of his or her total mental ability during a lifetime. This means that all persons have untapped mental resources that have never been developed and used.

Second, the first environment that a human occupies—the uterus—plays a significant part in the future development of intelligent capabilities. Conditions during pregnancy can seriously affect the development of the fetus in every way, including its brain and neural development. Lack of proper nutrition, intrauterine pressures, illness of the mother, physical and psychological trauma, parental chromosome damage as a result of drug use, and a host of other possibilities can damage the developing fetus and consequently place congenital limitations on an inherited brain structure.

Third, the home, the school, and the community environments of the developing child will also affect the development of potential mental abilities. Lack of love, lack of interaction with other people, and lack of nutritional foods can all inhibit the individual's intellectual and mental development. In reverse, an enriched and balanced environment can enhance and promote the development of mental abilities. In this sense, environment does have an effect upon intelligence as it is measured. But can intelligence be raised?

The answer to this is that every person does indeed possess an upper or outside limit of capability beyond which he or she cannot pass. However, since we know that the full mental capacity of the brain is never tapped, there are many things that can be done, particularly with children, to assist in the development and use of brain capacity.

The first environment is crucial. In order to ensure a healthy fetus and an uncomplicated birth, the mother needs to have the proper diet and to avoid the ingestion of drugs, alcohol, cigarette smoke, and other substances known to be potentially harmful to the developing fetus. Further, the pregnant woman should be under the care of a physician for the purpose of regular check-ups for weight control, body-fluid control, recommended regular exercise, and so on. It is also important that the mother be in good physical and mental health before the pregnancy occurs. These general guidelines are important not only for the health of the mother but as insurance that the unborn child has the best opportunity for normal and full development.

The best source for specific information is your physician and local public health agency.

You can promote optimal mental development in a child from the earliest stages of infancy. Stimulate equal development of both hemispheres of the brain by changing the infant's position frequently so that he or she views the room from all angles. You want to avoid development of a super-dominant hemisphere which might later inhibit interaction of the two hemispheres.

Talk to the developing infant. As the child begins to explore its environment through holding, touching, and pointing to objects, verbally identify the objects, as "chair," "flower," etc. Constant exposure to language and its meaning helps to develop the child's verbal ability, a very important aspect of high intelligence.

Give the child warmth, love, and acceptance. Never spank or punish an infant for behavior you think is unacceptable. Babies have no concept of right or wrong and cannot even tell the difference between their own inside world and the outside world in general. Anger or harsh punishment can have no positive effects on infant behavior but can cause emotional distress that may result in high anxiety, uncertainty, and even lack of self-identity in the developing ego. On the contrary, babies must receive attention for attention's sake alone and must receive recognition for their accomplishments so that they do not develop the idea that misbehavior is the only way to get attention.

Provide the child with a nutritious, varied diet. Avoid excessive processed sugar. Processed sugar seems to be related to hyperactivity and decreased concentration in children. Although total prohibition is unnecessary in the normal, healthy child, limiting sweets is an easy way to eliminate sugar's interference in behavior and development. Common sense and balance are the keys to diet, along with any vitamin or mineral supplements that the child's doctor or clinic advises. A healthy, active mind must be housed in the healthy, active body of which it is a part.

Do not force the child to use one hand rather than the other. The child will probably show preference for either the left or right hand, and it is very important to balanced mental functioning that this natural dominancy be honored. Interference may result in the interruption of normal development of mental processing efficiencies that in turn can adversely affect the development of reading and writing skills.

Provide play objects appropriate to learning at the child's age level. Since young children learn through movement and manipulation, play activities must be appropriate to muscle development. Development progresses from large-muscle to smaller muscle to eye–hand coordination. Play objects that are inappropriate to developmental level will only frustrate enjoyment and learning. In other words, very small children should be encouraged to climb and tumble, then to construct with sturdy, large blocks long before they are expected to handle even large-piece picture puzzles. Play objects should also encourage the child to imagine and to pretend. Imaginative play is the basis for later symbolization in language development. Imaginative play also helps the development of the creative right-brain processes of the mind. Toys that do not have a specific, rigidly defined purpose are best. Certainly expensive toys are unnecessary; pots, pans, boxes, yarn balls, and such are all excellent play objects.

Encourage and provide opportunity for physical play and exercise. As a child grows from infancy into the preschool years, blocks, puzzles, crayons, and large picture books provide practice for small-muscle, eye–hand, creativity, and preconceptual development. Show the child a picture—something which relates to the child's level and experience—and have the child tell you what he or she thinks is happening, or make up a story about it, or name the colors or the objects, and so on. Help the child see more than what was originally obvious, but not lots more. Good learning and development occur in cupfuls, not large buckets.

Play word and imagination games with the child, such as:

1.   Patty-cake and peek-a-boo with babies

2.   Hide-and-seek with toddlers

3. "I'm thinking of something round in this room . . ." with 3- to 5-year-olds. Add to the complexity as the child becomes more agile and speedy in arriving at answers.

4. Play Twenty Questions with elementary school children. You have something in mind or a number in mind. The child gets to ask no more than twenty questions in trying to guess what it is. Young children will take wild guesses, but they will develop and can learn "strategies" for good questions. For example, if you are thinking of a number, they will learn to ask such things as: "Is it odd or even?" "Is it under fifty?", and so on.

5. Play the automobile plate game as a family game. How quickly can one think of a phrase to go with three license plate letters? For example: SUS—sit up straight; IWL—I want lunch. This type of game can become quite hilarious, alleviating the tedium of travel while developing speed, agility, and creativity of mental processes.

You must provide structure for the child of any age but must allow for flexibility within that structure. Set standards of behavior but then allow for creative solutions of problems and for understanding of gradations and shadings, not rigid dichotomies of right or wrong, good or bad, early or late. Promote reinforcement of new ideas and new concepts by suggesting that the child express a thought or idea through media other than the first one of presentation. Art, crafts, drama, mime, and song are all acceptable media for the reinforcement of learning.

Encourage creativity by prizing individuality, independence, and risk taking. Discipline and tame that creativity by prizing sharing and cooperation and personal responsibility.

And what about the adult I.Q.? The adult I.Q. is not as amenable to enhancement as that of a child. One reason is that the neural connections in the brain are pretty well complete by the age of 16 or 17. Another reason is that thinking and learning styles and attitudes are fairly well developed and are a part of the total personality by the time a person reaches adulthood. But, although I.Q. itself cannot be improved, level of performance is another matter. The fact that stroke victims who lose speech or partial control of their bodies can sometimes be retrained for effective functioning is a tribute to the undeveloped potential of the brain even in adults. The inherited level of intelligence cannot be increased in either child or adult, but the undeveloped and unused abilities within that inherited structure can be tapped, developed, and enhanced.

As an adult's life becomes more complex and more demanding, certain mental activities no longer become part of the daily routine. These can be resurrected and redeveloped with practice.

Puzzles provide a special kind of challenge and fascination and a painless route towards rekindling old skills and abilities. As skill with puzzles increases, proficiency with words, numbers, three-dimensional relationships, etc. may progress well beyond the peak reached during youth and the years of schooling. Crossword puzzles and other word puzzles are unparalleled aids for building vocabulary and word fluency; number puzzles serve to enhance skill at computation and calculation and to encourage successful recognition of relationships among numbers; jigsaw puzzles and three-dimensional puzzles expand the ability to visualize relationships in space. Increasing competence with one type of puzzle will not automatically make one more competent at another type of puzzle, but fascination with puzzles will lead the curious adult from one kind to the next, with consequent growth of abilities in other mental activities.

To improve your functional I.Q., the intelligence level at which you actually perform (not your measured I.Q.), you will find that reading and developing greater awareness of worlds other than your own is a superb mind-expanding activity. Read magazines and books, nonfiction and fiction, on topics of interest to you—travel, other cultures, art, archeology, science, technology, etc. Read anything that provides new kinds of information and insights into life in general. Expanding your scope of interest and base of knowledge will not only increase your level of mental functioning but will make life more interesting and will make you more interesting as well.

Be positive. Use the "I can" rather than the "I can't" approach. Try, practice, develop a skill, ability, or interest to its fullest degree. Take the time to learn about or to learn how to do something that has been a secret ambition for a long time. One of the differences between the highly intelligent and the less intelligent is persistence and action. Intelligent, productive people are those who *do*, while others consider; they are people who try, while others give up; they are people who are willing to fail and try again, while others insist on first-time success.

Applying these ideas and principles will not turn you into a genius, unless you are a genius in disguise, but they will improve your attitudes, your general abilities, and your capacity for learning and will certainly make life more interesting and more personally satisfying.

Giftedness/Talent and Intelligence

Observing for Indicators of Giftedness and Talent

Although the first intelligence tests were designed in an effort to identify youngsters who were mentally handicapped, the group of children around whom interest is currently focused is that of the gifted and talented. High intelligence test scores are but one of many indicators that a person has potential or demonstrated abilities that are clearly outstanding. A high I.Q. is an indication of giftedness and talent in academic and intellectual areas, but in addition to academic giftedness, there are other areas of human endeavor and accomplishment in which a person may also be gifted. This fact, which has long been recognized by people working with children, was significant in influencing the research and studies of creativity which began in the late 1950s and early 1960s.

A person may be gifted and talented in one or more of four areas. These are:

1. **Academic (intellectual intelligence):** The academically gifted person demonstrates outstanding potential and/or achievement in those things which require mastery of a set of formalized symbols, such as language, or numbers, or both. This type of giftedness is reflected through I.Q. scores, subject area achievement scores, and academic or school marks.

2. **Creative:** The creatively gifted person demonstrates potential and/or achievement in those areas which require open, original, and uniquely productive thinking or action. Creativity can be demonstrated through the visual or performing arts, in academic areas, business or politics or in the social arena. There are tests which measure creativity, but, as previously stated, these have limitations, particularly in the difficulty of giving them to large groups of people. One of the best

ways to identify creativity is on the basis of behaviors which indicate creative thinking and performance.

3. **Psychomotor (physical):** The physically gifted person demonstrates outstanding potential and/or performance in activities requiring large-muscle, small-muscle, and eye–hand coordination. This includes such things as sports, dance, mechanics, rhythm, and the skills required for mastering the use of fine arts media. Outstanding psychomotor abilities can also be measured on the basis of observation.

4. **Social/Personal/Leadership:** The person with a gift for leadership demonstrates outstanding potential and/or performance in the areas of social and personal abilities required for leadership. These abilities can be measured through observation of daily behavior and are based upon personality characteristics, communication abilities, and leadership skills.

I.Q. scores are not valid indicators of abilities in creative, psychomotor, and leadership areas. How, then, can individuals who are gifted in these areas be identified? The best way to positively identify these individuals is to observe their behavior on a regular basis and to keep a log of the incidence of behaviors which have over time been singled out as reliable indicators of giftedness and talent.

You can arrive at a fairly accurate idea of the extent of any person's giftedness and talent by observing the person's general behavior on a regular basis. In addition, there are certain behaviors exhibited by infants and preschool children that are indicators of general levels of intelligence. We can easily identify highly intelligent children by comparing their performance with average or expected levels of performance of members of the general population at the same age. The following case histories will give you an idea of the ways in which some giftedly intelligent and creative persons have behaved as children.

TERRI is now a young adult. She drank unassisted from a cup at the age of four months; cut her first teeth at five and one-half months; walked at 10 months; talked in simple sentences (one, two words) at 10 and one-half months. She dressed and undressed herself with equal ease by 14 months, and was putting puzzles together and scribbling by the age of 18 months. She played cooperatively with other children the summer she was two. She was extremely social and competitive and was commonly the leader of the group.

Her outstanding physical coordination and willingness to take risks were apparent by age 18 months when she was found standing on top of the backyard swing set. Her mother gave her directions to help her get down, took her to the store and purchased sneakers, then showed her how to climb safely up and safely down. She could swim well by the age of three and a half.

Before entering kindergarten she composed lengthy and complicated stories and free-verse poetry and could add and subtract fractions in her head. Her individuality, willingness to take risks, conceptual maneuvers, and originality were highly encouraged by her family. She could write her name and numbers before entering school but was not taught to read. She was surrounded by and was exposed to a multitude of books and stories and was read to on a daily basis by her father and sometimes by her mother. The decision to not teach her to read was purposeful, as the school system she was entering was not prepared for a child who could already read at kindergarten entry.

As a fourth grader, Terri was the leader of a student protest against the teacher's methods of instruction. Her mother had discovered her at ten o'clock at night underneath her blankets with a flashlight writing spelling words ten times each. Surprised, because Terri was already reading above a tenth-grade level, her mother asked why Terri couldn't spell the words on the fourth-grade list. Terri informed her that she could indeed spell the words but that everyone had to write the words ten times whether they could spell them or not. Her mother reacted instantly with: "That's the dumbest thing I ever heard. Are you sure?" Terri was indeed sure, but was further informed to get her work done in the future before ten o'clock P.M. A few days later Terri nonchalantly informed her mother that she had to stay after school. When asked why, she answered that there was a fourth-grade protest and the teacher had asked all the youngsters who were involved in signing the petition to come in after school. Terri had of course written the petition and elicited the signatures of most of the class. The petition said: "We think that we should not have to write our spelling words ten times each when we already know how to spell them, and my mother thinks it is dumb." It was signed by Terri and eighteen others. Terri won her case on the basis of the logic and procedures used. The teacher, who had never really thought about this traditional and foolish method of teaching spelling, decided that it was indeed "dumb" and agreed that words which could be spelled before the beginning of the unit did not have to be written ten times each.

Terri excelled academically until the fifth grade, when she explained at home that she had found it unrewarding to do all her work as fast and as well as she could because the teacher only gave her more of the same.

Terri's academic success in high school was not outstanding. She graduated at the bottom of the top third of her class, but excelled in sports, language-related subjects, and art. She also should have received a letter of commendation for sociability and personality. Her I.Q. has been tested as 150 +, but she lost her interest in academic subjects at an early age because no real challenge was provided for her. Along with the development of some fine art skills, she also learned to play two musical instruments with highly competent, but not talented, performance.

Terri grew up in a family where there was high educational attainment, but where independence, individuality, and openness were prized over the conformity and social acceptance which are more likely to be valued in families of high academic achievers.

BETH reported having memories from the age of one. This is highly unusual in most individuals, even in highly sensitive and intelligent persons. She talked at an early age and could carry on a conversation with detail and fluency of language by age three. Her friends were usually older, and she was an accepted part of the adult world from a preschool age. Her powers of observation and memory were unique and her ability to group and classify as a preschooler was evidenced by the fact that she could identify by make and model any automobile she saw by age four. By age four she also could write her name and numbers and use numerical concepts, identify 48 different colors, and understand the sequence of hours in the day. She took dancing lessons at age four and was extremely well coordinated, advancing to an older class quite rapidly.

In school she achieved extremely high marks and could read seven grades above her third-grade level. Her achievement in other school subjects was three or more grades above level. She was a varsity athlete for four years in both high school and college and participated in every extracurricular activity available. She learned to play three musical instruments, two self-taught, and learned the rudiments of several others. She received several scholarships to college and was later offered scholarships to both law school and art school.

Beth's I.Q. has been measured from 130 to 145. She is both creative and intelligent and has attained high educational status and professional accomplishment as an adult. Her interest in music has continued as a hobby, and she also performs with a professional group.

These persons—Terri and Beth—could easily have been identified as being both intelligent and creative before they entered school purely on the basis of the kinds of things they did in comparison to other children of the same age. Beth's high academic achievement in comparison to Terri's is related to inner motivation, the level of personal rewards received, and the family structure in which she grew up. Beth's family allowed and encouraged independence and nonconformity in the home, but there was a strong emphasis on social acceptance and conformity in the community.

Milestones in Infant and Preschool Development

By comparing the milestone events of regular child development, such as sitting up, talking, walking, and so on, you can determine if a child shows potential for high, average, or low levels of performance in later academic and creative pursuits. The following list charts some of these important developmental behaviors and activities by the age at which one can generally expect a child to have mastered each one. These ages are based on averages. The actual behavior might appear a few weeks (in infancy) to a few months (in a preschool child) before or after the age indicated. If a child accomplishes a large number of these milestone activities a significant period of time before average expectancy, it is a good indicator of high potential.

Infancy (Birth to 2 Years)

3 months: can support self on forearms while lying on stomach and has fairly good control of head; can hold objects in fist and put in mouth; smiles, babbles, coos; turns head toward sounds; recognizes familiar persons; shows an interest in the surroundings.

6 to 7 months: can roll over; can pick up objects and can transfer from one hand (fist) to another; first teeth appear; can laugh aloud; puts out arms to be held; babbles in response to adult talk; begins to repeat a meaningful sound such as *ma* or *da*; looks for objects out of sight and for the source of sounds.

9 to 10 months: can sit up without help; can pull self to standing position; creeps; picks up objects with thumb and index finger; can hold own bottle; can play simple game, such as pattycake (clap hands); smiles at self in mirror; offers objects to others, but doesn't let go; imitates sounds, facial expressions, and gestures; responds to own name; understands "bye-bye" and "no-no"; shows interest in picture books.

12 months: can walk with help, or perhaps alone; lets go of objects offered; shows preference for left or right hand; likes being the center of attention; comes when called; helps dress self; has own jargon, plus one other word; shakes head "no"; expresses emotion.

18 months: walks up stairs with help; walks on level ground unassisted; turns pages of book, two or three at a time; feeds self with spoon; plays alone when in company of other children; wants to explore surroundings; may have security object, such as blanket or thumb; follows simple directions; has vocabulary of six to ten words; points to objects wanted or named by others; imitates adult activities, such as sweeping, dusting.

Preschool (2 to 5 Years)

2 years: can walk up and down stairs; can hold cup with one hand; runs without falling; turns pages in book, one at a time; scribbles; plays parallel with other children; asks to go to toilet; speaks in short sentences; uses pronouns, *me* and *mine*; obeys simple commands; begins to understand time; has vocabulary of 200 to 300 words.

2½ years: throws objects overhand; jumps in place; holds pencil or crayon like an adult; begins to play with other children; says "no" to just about everything in effort to show independence; can give first and last name if asked; uses *I*; uses plurals and past tenses.

3 years: can pedal tricycle, swing, and climb; alternates feet when going up and down stairs; dresses and undresses self; begins to use scissors; shares and takes turns; finds ways of getting own way; tells short stories; repeats a few numbers; knows own sex; begins to ask "Why?"; is very self-centered; can think about own behavior; has vocabulary of about 900 words.

4 years: tries to skip and hop; brushes teeth; can catch a ball; can button clothes; can alternate feet going both up and down stairs; tells "pretend" stories; shows off; has sense of *mine* and *yours*; can recite poem or song from memory; knows basic colors; uses language with purpose; may use profanity; has vocabulary of about 1,500 words; learns some number concepts; understands simple cause and effect; begins to stop saying "no."

5 years: begins to add detail to drawings (but drawings not realistic in adult sense); dresses independently; jumps, climbs, and skips well; walks backward; is cooperative and sympathetic; minds; is trustworthy; is generous; talks *a lot*; uses conversation; asks for meaning of words; can copy a triangle; knows age and address; knows days of week; understands week as a period of time; can count to ten; has vocabulary of about 2,000 words; asks more questions than at any other age.

Checklist of Behaviors to Measure Giftedness and Talent

Gifted/talented persons tend to be above average in health, coordination, and the rate of both mental and physical development. Not only do they develop more quickly in mental and physical areas, but they also exhibit a greater complexity and power in the areas of noted development than others of average abilities.

Use the checklist which follows to measure yourself, another, or a child for indications of gifted and talented behavior. For each item listed, check:

1.   If the behavior is never seen (1 point)

2.   If the behavior is seldom seen (2 points)

3.   If the behavior is occasionally seen (3 points)

4.   If the behavior is seen fairly often (4 points)

5.   If the behavior occurs most of the time (5 points)

Checklist

	(1) never	(2) seldom	(3) occasionally	(4) often	(5) almost always
I. Intellectual Intelligence					
(AS A CHILD)					
1. Chooses older playmates	___	___	___	___	___
2. Gets along well with adults	___	___	___	___	___
3. Prefers adult company to that of peers	___	___	___	___	___
4. Enjoys reading biography/autobiography, reference books	___	___	___	___	___

	(1) never	(2) seldom	(3) occasionally	(4) often	(5) almost always
(ALL AGES)					
5. Curious and inquisitive					
6. Has large vocabulary					
7. Uses language fluently and richly					
8. Enjoys reading					
9. Has abundance of ideas					
10. Has excellent memory					
11. Has large bank of information					
12. Has sharp sense of time					
13. Learns quickly and easily					
14. Notes and uses detail					
15. Comes up with answers quickly, easily					
16. Answers are considered, appropriate					
17. Quickly understands cause–effect					
18. Likes school—likes learning					
19. Understands ideas quickly, easily					
20. Can apply learning from one situation to another					
21. Finishes tasks started					
22. Is well organized					
23. Has mental and physical energy					
24. Is industrious					
25. Has strong self-motivation					
26. Can work independently					
27. Is highly competitive					
28. Has high personal standards					

	(1) never	(2) seldom	(3) occasionally	(4) often	(5) almost always
29. Has strong sense of justice	——	——	————	——	————
30. Enjoys puzzles and mental games	——	——	————	——	————
31. Has common sense	——	——	————	——	————
32. Has (had) high school marks (over 90)	——	——	————	——	————

	below 90	90–109	110–119	120–129	130+
33. I.Q.	——	——	————	——	————

(If I.Q. is 150+, score 6 points) ————

Scores: 33–52 (low) ————

53–78 (average) ————

79–105 (bright) ————

106–132 (superior) ————

133–165 (gifted) ————

166 and over (super-gifted) ————

(See additional behaviors at end of checklist) ————

II. Creativity	(1) never	(2) seldom	(3) occasionally	(4) often	(5) almost always
1. Is flexible in thought and action	——	——	————	——	————
2. Can live and deal with uncertainty	——	——	————	——	————
3. Has profusion of ideas, solutions, etc.	——	——	————	——	————
4. Ideas, solutions, etc., are unique and original	——	——	————	——	————
5. Is personally independent	——	——	————	——	————
6. Is uninhibited	——	——	————	——	————
7. Is adventurous	——	——	————	——	————
8. Is inventive	——	——	————	——	————

	(1) never	(2) seldom	(3) occasionally	(4) often	(5) almost always
9. Fantasizes, daydreams					
10. Has rich imagination					
11. Uses a lot of elaboration and detail					
12. Is not afraid to be different					
13. Takes risks					
14. Questions the status quo					
15. Offers constructive criticism					
16. Offers constructive alternatives					
17. Concerned with changing, innovating, improving					
18. Is sensitive to beauty					
19. Is sensitive to other people					
20. Is very self-aware					
21. Is highly self-honest					
22. Has keen (and perhaps unusual) sense of humor					
23. May be outgoing or may be withdrawn, but has strong self-assurance in personal projects					
24. Emotionally stable					
(BUT AT TIMES MAY BE)					
25. excitable					
26. moody					
27. irritable (especially if interrupted during personal activities)					
28. Dislikes routine and repetition					
29. Likes to work toward goal, product					

	(1) never	(2) seldom	(3) occasionally	(4) often	(5) almost always
30. Can see the "whole" quickly					
31. Strong sense of proportion and balance (visually, mentally, physically)					
32. When given a choice, chooses activities requiring creative endeavor					

Scores: 32–47 (creativity inhibited) _____

48–75 (average creativity) _____

76–91 (above average creativity) _____

92–128 (superior creativity) _____

129–160 (creatively talented) _____

III. Social/Personal/Leadership

	(1) never	(2) seldom	(3) occasionally	(4) often	(5) almost always
1. Self-assertive					
2. Bored by routine					
3. Becomes absorbed and involved					
4. Interested in controversial, adult, or abstract problems					
5. Likes to organize					
6. Extremely concerned with morals, ethics					
7. Sets high goals					
8. Likes and takes responsibility					
9. Is popular, well-liked					
10. Gets along well with others					
11. Self-confident with all ages					
12. Adaptable to new situations					

	(1) never	(2) seldom	(3) occasionally	(4) often	(5) almost always
13. Flexible—can change ways of getting goals without frustration					
14. Sociable—prefers to be with others					
15. Genuine interest in other people					
16. Is initiator of activities					
17. A resource for others; they naturally turn for guidance, direction					
18. Is open to differences in others					
19. Participates in many social activities					
20. Is leader of the group					
21. Speaks easily and fluently					

Scores: 21–33 (definite follower) _____

34–49 (average social skills; not destined to lead) _____

50–66 (above average social leadership skills; may lead at times) _____

67–83 (superior social leadership skills) _____

84–105 (socially gifted; leadership skills) _____

	(1) never	(2) seldom	(3) occasionally	(4) often	(5) almost always
IV. Physical					
1. Shows excellent general health					
2. Shows superior physical strength					
3. Shows superior physical agility					
4. Shows superior physical balance					
5. Shows superior rhythm					
6. Is well coordinated					

	(1) never	(2) seldom	(3) occasionally	(4) often	(5) almost always
7. Is larger than average (child)	__	__	__	__	__
8. Has high energy and pep	__	__	__	__	__
9. Moves with exceptional ease and flow	__	__	__	__	__
10. Participates in sports and physical games	__	__	__	__	__
11. Would rather participate than watch	__	__	__	__	__

Scores: 11–17 (very low) _____

18–25 (low-average physical skills) _____

26–34 (strong-average physical skills) _____

35–43 (superior physical skills) _____

44–55 (gifted in psychomotor skills _____

Those persons who are clearly gifted and talented often are outstanding in more than one of the above areas. Total scores for overall giftedness and talent are:

97–151 (low range of abilities) _____

152–229 (average abilities) _____

231–299 (above-average abilities) _____

300–388 (superior abilities) _____

389–485 (gifted/talented) _____

485+ (super-giftedness/talent) _____

In addition to the general behaviors listed, give an extra point for each of the following, as observed in children or in the childhood of adults.

Intellectual Intelligence

1.   Teaches self to read before formal instruction
2.   Collects things
3.   Organizes and maintains collection
4.   1 point for each organized collection

5.   Maintains an interest or a hobby over a long period of time

6.   Uses scientific approach to thinking and problem solving (analytical, methodical)

Creativity (Visual Arts)

1.   Likes and uses color with originality
2.   Chooses art projects when given a choice
3.   Good sense of space and design
4.   Is sensitive to forms and shapes
5.   Sensitive to texture
6.   Uses a variety of line, texture, color, shape in artistic creations

Creativity (Music)

1.   Chooses music for activity when given choice
2.   Can match pitch easily
3.   Easily remembers a melody and can reproduce accurately
4.   Plays toy instruments at an early age
5.   Invents melodies
6.   Invents instruments
7.   Reads music easily

Physical (Dance)

1.   Responds to music with coordinated movement of body
2.   Can imitate gestures and movements with ease

Summary

Preschool children who are gifted and talented tend to develop earlier than their less-gifted peers in physical, mental, creative, and social skills, and their activities are beyond their age level not only in order of appearance, but also in the complexity and power of the demonstrated behavior. Contrary to what was once believed, highly gifted/talented individuals are also generally superior in health, strength, emotional stability, and sociability than less gifted persons. Whether or not these outstanding abilities are fully developed depends on parental attitudes and the types and numbers of learning opportunities that are available and prized, both in the home prior to entering school and during the school experience and in the school itself.

A child's intelligence will develop to its optimum potential only if the child is allowed to develop physically and emotionally and is encouraged to probe and question. A certain level of mental and emotional "tension" is productive to learning and achievement. The productive "tension" is significantly different from that in which anxiety is so high that mental activity and development are blocked and frozen.

In addition, all persons, regardless of intelligence or general abilities, do have talents and gifts in certain areas. These should be respected and nourished. The development of intelligence and creativity at all levels of performance requires structure in living which promotes the highest level of personal organization and the development of self-discipline. Highly intelligent and highly creative persons are able to provide more personal structure than the less gifted, but all need basic guidelines and rules for living.

Rigidity of rules will inhibit the growth of independence and exploration necessary for the development of intelligent, creative, physical, and social skills. On the other hand, over-permissiveness will promote equally nonproductive chaos. Common sense must rule as family guidelines are established, with reasonable allowances for variation in individual styles and requirements. However, all children—and even adults—have a basic need to know the limits of the rules and need consistency in application of the rules over a period of time.

PART
IV

Computer I.Q.

Intelligence and Computer Operation

Willing or not, we have arrived at the computer age. While this new era will bring forth its own host of problems and negatives, humanity now stands at one of the most exciting frontiers in history. Guided by human intelligence, the computer—with its lightning speed—will extend creativity a thousandfold to accomplishments previously undreamed of. Freed from the restrictions of time and labor which hitherto have consumed 90 percent of our time, we will for the first time be able to give total sweep to our inherent personal and collective genius.

Against the background of this exciting and rather awesome new future, where does the individual stand and how does he or she relate to it? To the vast majority of us—products of our industrial society and its values—the sudden appearance of the computer world confronts us with all the elements of future shock. It is at once exciting, mysterious, and—to the uninitiated—a little frightening. For the millions of us who have no knowledge or experience with this space-age phenomenon—but who realize that it will play a major role in our future—the anxious concerns that disturb each individual are apparent in the questions typically asked:

> "It looks so complicated—how will I ever learn to use one?"
> "I'm not a math or engineering whiz—isn't this just for the superbrains?"
> "I won't blow it up—will I? What if I make a mistake?"
> "How will I ever understand those weird marks and funny symbols?"
> "What possible use or good can I get from it?"

For anyone not familiar with computers, these are all valid questions. Rest assured, however, that despite its sophistication *anyone* of normal intelligence can operate and program a computer—and the uses to which the computer can be put are virtually endless.

Contrary to popular opinion, one does not have to be a math or engineering specialist to operate or program a computer. What is required, however, is logic and an attention to detail. In the computer world, there is no room for sloppy thinking; computing is literally an exercise in disciplined thinking and problem solving.

It is the objective of this chapter to give the reader an insight into his or her potential success in the operation and programming of computers by testing those elements essential in computer use, i.e., logic, reasoning, spatial visualization, and problem solving. The test will give the reader both an introduction to the computer world and a measure of his or her present capacity to use the new computer technology.

The successful operation of a computer depends primarily upon two specific factors: the ability of the individual to *precisely* follow *all* instructions and rules (syntax) and the ability to think and solve problems *logically*, using all aspects of intelligence to best advantage.

The following test has been specifically designed to test your ability to pay careful attention to rules and to think in a logical manner. The test consists of 50 questions.

Work rapidly and try to answer all questions within 50 minutes.

Computer Operator Test

Syntax Questions 1–20

All computer languages have a well-designed set of rules, known as *syntax*. Every rule must be carefully followed if you wish to relate to and use a computer. Language characters and syntax rules for any computer language are completely arbitrary, and you should not seek a rational explanation—just follow the rules as they are given.

You will be given a separate set of language characters and syntax rules for each specific set of ten questions. You will also be given a correct sample model for that specific language set for comparison. Check each series of characters to make certain that all of the syntax rules have been followed. If they have, mark "correct" (or just plain "C") in the answer column. If the series has not followed the syntax rules, mark it "incorrect" (or just plain "I") in the answer column. Below is a sample question.

Language Characters

Large set: (A, B, C, . . . Z)
Small set: (a, b, c, . . . z)
Number set: (0, 1, 2, 3, 4, 5, 6, 7, 8, 9)
Punctuation set: (+ – @ * = #.)

Syntax Rules

1. All punctuation marks must remain in their original positions.
2. There must be a period at the end of every series.
3. Large symbols cannot be placed next to each other.
4. No series can contain more than seven (7) characters.
5. Small set letter characters can be replaced by numbers.

Correct Sample Model: SbbR = N

Questions	Answers	Questions	Answers
1 S22Q = P.	Correct (C)	3 B44OR – M.	Incorrect (I)
2 S45R*7	Incorrect (I)	4 S66N#Q.	Correct (C)

Since question 1 followed all of the syntax rules, we marked "correct" in the answer column. Questions 2 and 3 violated one or more of the rules, so we marked them both "incorrect" in the answer column. Question 4 followed all rules, so we marked it "correct."

In the following test questions, follow the same procedure, checking to see whether or not all of the syntax rules have been followed, and then mark the questions correct or incorrect according to your determination.

Begin the test.

Language Character Set #1

Large set: (A, B, C, . . . Z)
Small set: (0, 1, 2, 3, . . . 9)
Punctuation: (# = / $ ¢)

Syntax Rules

1. A / must end all series.
2. Each series must start with the next letter in the alphabet according to the first letter of the preceding series.
3. When two large characters are next to each other, the second can be replaced with a character of the small set.
4. Only 5 may not be placed next to itself.
5. Except for 5, the same small character may not be used twice in the same series.

Correct Sample Model: A1AA#2/

(Mark "C" for Correct or
"I" for Incorrect)

	Questions	Answers
1	B3R2/1/	
2	C6RP$6/	
3	D2L2¢31	
4	E1GZ=4/	
5	G4Q3#71	
6	H5Z3=8/	
7	I8N4$2/	
8	J7ER$1/	
9	K9B2#4/	
10	L0FG#7/	

Language Character Set #2

Large set: (A, B, C, . . . Z)
Small set: (a, b, c, . . . z)
Punctuation: (+ − @ * .)

Syntax Rules

1. Numbers cannot be used in this series.
2. A period must end all series.
3. A series can have as many as but no more than 7 characters, including punctuation.

4. Large, small, and punctuation characters must remain in the same position given in the sample model.
5. Small double characters must be replaced by consecutive letters of the alphabet.

Correct Sample Model: AabA*A.

(Mark "C" for Correct or "I" for Incorrect)

	Questions	Answers
11	CCdR+S.	
12	PuvN@T.	
13	FghU+M.	
14	ErsX*L.	
15	GhjS–A*	
16	AaaA*A–	
17	HdeO@Rs.	
18	BbcD@7.	
19	cLMN.Q.	
20	ShiPPd.	

Problem Analysis Questions 21–40

Each of the following questions contains a simple problem that will test your ability to evaluate a given situation and arrive at a logical answer. None of the problems involves any complex math, but all of them do force you to think analytically.

Sample Problem

A library charges 10¢ for each of the first five days and 3¢ for each additional day that a book is overdue. If John paid $1.10 in late charges, how many days overdue was the book?

28	25	29	16	24
(a)	(b)	(c)	(d)	(e)

Solution

If the charge was 10¢ per day for the first five days, then the charge for those first five days was 50¢. Since John paid a total of $1.10, then minus the 50¢, he paid 60¢ for the remaining days. At 3¢ for each additional day, 60¢ would have covered the cost for an additional 20 days. 20 days plus the first 5 days is a total of 25 days. Therefore you would have picked "B" as the correct answer.

Begin the test. Circle the letter below your answer.

---

21. Mrs. Jones and her daughter Sally made 126 sandwiches for the local church supper. Mrs. Jones made 6 more than twice as many sandwiches as Sally. How many sandwiches did Mrs. Jones make?

92	82	78	86	84
(a)	(b)	(c)	(d)	(e)

22. A shoe factory turns out S pairs of shoes per hour. How many minutes does it take to make a pair of shoes?

$60\,S$	$\frac{60}{S}$	$\frac{S}{60}$	$60\,\frac{S}{100}$	$2\,\frac{S}{60}$
(a)	(b)	(c)	(d)	(e)

23. The weight of the contents of a can of corn is 1 lb. 4 oz. How many ounces do the contents of a case of 24 cans weigh?

480	540	360	240	400
(a)	(b)	(c)	(d)	(e)

24. The area of a square is expressed as A = LW. If L, length, and W, width, are each multiplied by two, the area would be

Twice as large.	The same.	Eight times as large.
(a)	(b)	(c)
Four times as large.		None of the above.
(d)		(e)

25. Fred picked twice as many watermelons as George, and Harry picked as many as Fred and George together. If the total number of watermelons picked by all three was 120, how many did George pick?

40	60	10	20	30
(a)	(b)	(c)	(d)	(e)

26. The price of an article was cut 20% for a sale. By what percent must the item be increased to again sell the article at the original price?

15%	20%	25%	30%	40%
(a)	(b)	(c)	(d)	(e)

27. Mr. Johnson is on a weekly salary of $140.00 as a store salesman. In addition, he receives a commission of $\frac{1}{2}$% on his weekly sales. Last week his sales were $6600.00 How much did he earn last week?

$182.50	$166.00	$173.00	$178.50	$206.00
(a)	(b)	(c)	(d)	(e)

28. Mary had a number of cookies. After eating one, she gave half the remainder to her sister. After eating another cookie, she gave half of what was left to her brother. Mary now had only five cookies left. How many cookies did she start with?

11	22	23	45	46
(a)	(b)	(c)	(d)	(e)

29. It takes 9 men 17 days to complete a certain construction job. How many days will it take if only 2 men, working at the same rate, have to do the job?

$70 \frac{1}{2}$	64	$82 \frac{1}{2}$	68	$76 \frac{1}{2}$
(a)	(b)	(c)	(d)	(e)

30. John received $.41 change from a purchase in the drugstore. If he received six coins, three of the coins had to be:

Pennies	Nickels	Dimes	Quarters	Half-dollars
(a)	(b)	(c)	(d)	(e)

31. George and Harry together earn $2100 per month. If George earns three-quarters as much as Harry, what is two-thirds of George's monthly salary?

$500	$700	$600	$1200	$900
(a)	(b)	(c)	(d)	(e)

32. A rectangle is 2W feet wide. Its length is 5 times longer than its width. What is the area of that rectangle?

$5 \times 2W$	$5W + 2W$	$2W (5 \times 2W)$
(a)	(b)	(c)

$\dfrac{2W}{5} \times \dfrac{5W}{2}$	$WW + 5W$
(d)	(e)

33. 40% of a 15 lb. soil mixture is peat moss. How many pounds of the remaining mixture is sand and humus?

10 lbs.	9 lbs.	8 lbs.	7 lbs.	6 lbs.
(a)	(b)	(c)	(d)	(e)

34. Sally can type 5 letters in 20 minutes, Marge can type 3 letters in 20 minutes, and Gloria can type 2 letters in 10 minutes. Working together, how many minutes will it take them to type 36 letters?

45	70	60	54	67
(a)	(b)	(c)	(d)	(e)

35. Tom and Jerry start from the same point and walk in opposite directions. Tom walks at the rate of 5 miles an hour and Jerry walks at the rate of 7 miles an hour. How many miles apart will they be at the end of $4\frac{1}{2}$ hours?

50	45	48	54	46
(a)	(b)	(c)	(d)	(e)

36. Two men decide to drive to a distant city and will take the same road. The first one leaves 2 hours ahead of the second one and drives at 40 miles an hour, while the second one drives at 60 miles an hour. How many hours will it take the second man to catch up with the first one?

5	6	10	4	2
(a)	(b)	(c)	(d)	(e)

37. A young man on his bicycle rode 30 miles at a speed of 15 miles per hour. At how many miles per hour would he have to travel coming back if he wished to average 20 miles per hour for the round trip?

15	30	25	20	35
(a)	(b)	(c)	(d)	(e)

38. A 6-ft. tree casts a shadow 8 ft. long. A second tree standing nearby casts a shadow 36 ft. long. How high is the second tree?

42 ft.	24 ft.	18 ft.	27 ft.	32 ft.
(a)	(b)	(c)	(d)	(e)

39. Five boarders at a local boardinghouse pay a total of $125.00 per week. How much will 13 boarders pay at the same rate?

$325	$290	$350	$300	$375
(a)	(b)	(c)	(d)	(e)

40. Twenty soldiers at an advance camp had food supplies sufficient for 45 days. They were joined by 10 more soldiers who had no food supplies. How many days will the overall food supplies last the 30 soldiers now in the camp?

35	30	40	32	38
(a)	(b)	(c)	(d)	(e)

Procedure Analysis Questions 41–50

In operating a computer, you must follow the procedure of a program in a logical manner. In the following questions you will be given a series of flow charts for various simple programs and asked to determine the logical sequence of steps in the procedure of the program. Following are sample questions.

Program Procedure

The temperature of a room must be kept between 65° and 75°.

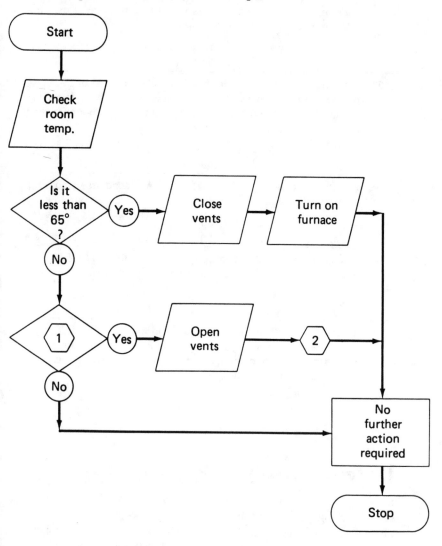

Sample Questions

A   No. 1 in the diagram asks which question?
   (a)   What is room temperature?
   (b)   Is it less than 75°?
   (c)   Is it more than 75°?
   (d)   Close vents?

The best answer for the above question is "C" because the temperature must be kept between 65° and 75°.

B   What directions would best fit in No. 2?
   (a)   Close vents.
   (b)   Open door.
   (c)   Turn on furnace.
   (d)   Turn off furnace.

The best answer for the above question is "D" because the room is too hot and the furnace must be shut off.

In the test questions following, you will similarly go through each program procedure and answer the questions asked.

Program Procedure

Returning Jon Smith's call.

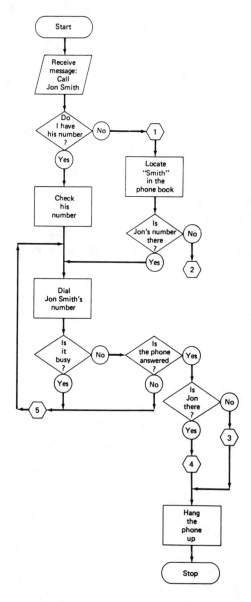

41. The best answer for No. 1 is:

    (a) Wail till Jon calls.
    (b) Get the phone book.
    (c) Try several numbers.
    (d) Call someone who knows Jon's number.

42. The best answer for No. 2 is:

    (a) Wait till Jon calls.
    (b) Get the phone book.
    (c) Call operator to find if he has a new listing.
    (d) Locate his mailing address.

43. The best answer for No. 3 is:

    (a) Ask for Jon's mailing address.
    (b) Leave a message for Jon.
    (c) Give up trying to call Jon.
    (d) Call the operator.

44. The best answer for No. 4 is:

    (a) Give Jon the message.
    (b) Ask Jon for his mailing address.
    (c) Talk with Jon.
    (d) Ask him to please hold.

45. The best answer for No. 5 is:

    (a) Call the operator.
    (b) Wail till Jon calls.
    (c) Try another number.
    (d) Wait 15 minutes and call again.

Program Procedure

Assume you are going to use the car today and you always keep the gas tank at least half full.

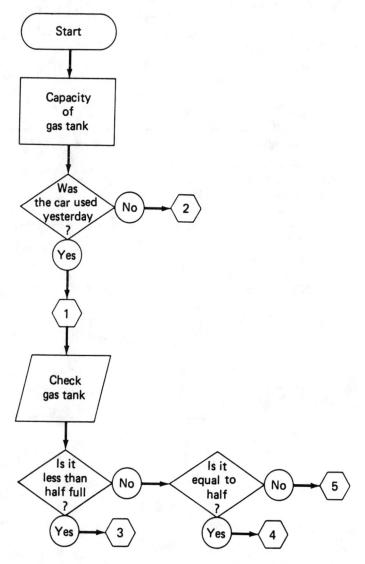

46. No. 1 means:

   (a) The tank is empty.
   (b) The tank may need to be filled.
   (c) The car does not need gas.
   (d) The tires need to be inflated.

47. No. 2 means:

   (a) The tank is probably not empty.
   (b) The oil should be checked.
   (c) You should not use your car.
   (d) Your car needs to be tuned.

48. No. 3 means:

   (a) The tank is empty.
   (b) The car does not need gas.
   (c) Definitely fill the tank.
   (d) The tires need to be inflated.

49. No. 4 means:

   (a) The tank is empty.
   (b) The car does not need gas.
   (c) You have a choice, to fill or not to fill the tank.
   (d) Add dry gas to the tank.

50. No. 5 means:

   (a) The tank is over half full.
   (b) The tank is empty.
   (c) Definitely fill the tank.
   (d) You need to add dry gas.

Test Answers
Computer Operator Test

1. **C**	11. **I**	21. **D**	31. **C**	41. **B**
2. **I**	12. **C**	22. **B**	32. **C**	42. **C**
3. **I**	13. **C**	23. **A**	33. **B**	43. **B**
4. **C**	14. **C**	24. **D**	34. **C**	44. **C**
5. **I**	15. **I**	25. **D**	35. **D**	45. **D**
6. **C**	16. **I**	26. **C**	36. **D**	46. **B**
7. **C**	17. **I**	27. **C**	37. **B**	47. **A**
8. **C**	18. **I**	28. **C**	38. **D**	48. **C**
9. **C**	19. **I**	29. **E**	39. **A**	49. **C**
10. **C**	20. **I**	30. **C**	40. **B**	50. **A**

Answers and Explanations

1. **C** This character series follows all syntax rules.
2. **I** This series violates the syntax rule which prohibits two small characters in the same series. The small character 6 is used twice.
3. **I** Series violates two syntax rules: (1) not using "/" at the end of the series, and (2) using a small character (2) twice.
4. **C** All syntax rules followed.
5. **I** Series violates two syntax rules: (1) not ending series in "/", and (2) not starting series with "F," the next letter of the alphabet following "E," the first letter of the preceding series.
6. **C** All syntax rules followed.
7. **C** All syntax rules followed.
8. **C** All syntax rules followed.
9. **C** All syntax rules followed.
10. **C** All syntax rules followed.
11. **I** Second small character in the series (a) has been replaced by a large character (C) which violates the rule that all size characters must remain in the same position as the model.

12. **C** All syntax rules followed.
13. **C** All syntax rules followed.
14. **C** All syntax rules followed.
15. **I** Violates all but the first of the syntax rules.
16. **I** Violates two rules: rule (2) and rule (5).
17. **I** Violates two syntax rules: (1) the 7-character limitation (series has 8), and (2) position rule for large and small characters.
18. **I** Violates syntax rule (1), numbers cannot be used (series contains a 7).
19. **I** First, second, and third characters of the series violate the position rule.
20. **I** First, fifth, and sixth characters of the series violate the position rule.
21. **D** Sally made X number of sandwiches and her mother made 2X + 6 sandwiches. Total was 126 sandwiches, so—

$$
\begin{array}{rcl}
3X + 6 & = & 126 \\
-6 & & -6 \\
\hline
3X & = & 120 \\
X & = & 40
\end{array}
$$

Therefore Sally's mother made 2 × 40 + 6, or 86, sandwiches.

22. **B** If we divide the total number of shoes made per hour (S) into 60 minutes, we will find out how many minutes it takes to make a pair of shoes.
23. **A** There are 16 ounces in a pound. So 1 lb., 4 oz. is 20 ounces.
$$20 \times 24 = 480$$
24. **D** Let us say that L = 2 and W is 4. 2 × 4 = 8. If we double these values, i.e., to L = 4 and W = 8, we get a quadrupling effect: 4 × 8 = 32 (which is 4 times greater than 8).
25. **D** George picked X number of watermelons and Fred picked twice as many, or 2X. Harry picked as many as both of the other two, or 3X. Together, they picked 6X watermelons. Since

$$6X = 120$$
$$X = 20$$

George, therefore, picked 20 watermelons.

26. **C** A $1.00 item, for example, if reduced 20%, will sell for 80¢. To sell it at $1.00 again, you must increase the price 20¢. 20¢ is 25% of 80¢.

27. **C** 1% of $6600 is $66.00. $\frac{1}{2}$% would be half of this—or $33.00 $33.00 + $140.00 is $173.00.

28. **C** Mary had 5 cookies left after giving an equal number to her brother, so she had 10 cookies before sharing. She had just eaten cookie number 11. Right before eating number 11, she had shared equally with her sister, so she had 22 cookies. She ate one before she started to share, so began with 23 cookies.

29. **E** Since 9 men provide 4 $\frac{1}{2}$ times as much labor as 2 men (9 ÷ 2), then it will also take 4 $\frac{1}{2}$ times as long (17 × 4 $\frac{1}{2}$), which comes to 76$\frac{1}{2}$ days.

30. **C** 3 dimes, 2 nickels, and 1 penny is the only possible solution.

31. **C** Let 3X represent George's salary and 4X represent Harry's salary. Then 7X = $2100, and X = $300. Therefore Harry's salary (4X) = $1200, George's salary (3X) = $900. $\frac{2}{3}$ of $900 = $600.

32. **C** Area of a rectangle is length × width. If the width is 2W and the length is 5 times the width, or 5 × 2W, then the area is 2W (5 × 2W).

33. **B** 40% of 15 lbs. is 6 lbs. Therefore, the balance of the mixture would weigh 9 lbs.

34. **C** If Gloria can type 2 letters in 10 minutes, she can type 4 letters in 20 minutes. Therefore in 20 minutes, the three girls can type a total of 12 letters (4 + 5 + 3). So to type 36 letters (3 times as many) will take 3 times as long, or 60 minutes.

35. **D** Since Tom and Jerry are walking in opposite directions, their rates of speed are combined to 12 mph (5 + 7).
$$12 \times 4\frac{1}{2} = 54.$$

36. **D** The first man @ 40 miles per hour will be ahead by a distance of 80 miles (40 × 2) when the second man starts out. Since he is traveling @ 60 mph—20 mph faster—he will close the gap of 80 miles at the rate of 20 miles per hour, for a total of 4 hours.
$$80 \div 20 = 4.$$

37. **B** The total round trip was 60 miles (30 each way). @ 20 mph, it would take 3 hrs. (60 ÷ 20 = 3). However, it took

the rider 2 hrs. (@ 15 mph) going just one way. Therefore he would have to cover the return trip in one hr. (or 30 mph) to average 20 mph on the entire round trip.

38. **D**
$$6:8 = X:36$$
$$8X = 6(36) \text{ or } 216$$
$$X = 216 \div 8 \text{ or } 27$$

39. **A** If 5 boarders pay a total of $125.00 per week, then each pays $25.00 per week. Therefore 13 boarders would pay 13 × $25, or $325.00 per week.

40. **B** 10 new soldiers represent $\frac{1}{3}$ of the total of 30 soldiers now in camp, and original supplies will thus be consumed $\frac{1}{3}$ faster, or in 30 days instead of 45 days.

41. **B** Jon is waiting for us to call, so A is not a good choice. C and D are possibilities, but we should try the phone book first.

42. **C** A is still not a good choice, and we've already tried B. D is a possibility if no other option exists. Calling is the most logical next step.

43. **B** Our basic purpose was to return Jon's call. Leaving a message is the best and quickest way of letting him know that we have done so.

44. **C** Talking to Jon about his call is the basic purpose of ours. The other actions are illogical.

45. **D** Answer B is a possibility, but it would be more considerate if we honored Jon's request and kept trying to reach him.

46. **B** Answers A and C are absolute assumptions that cannot be made. D is a possibility, but is not as relevant to our purpose as is answer B.

47. **A** Answers B and D are irrelevant to our purpose and C is contrary to our intention to use the car.

48. **C** This agrees with our program procedure.

49. **C** Since the condition agrees with the program procedure, i.e., that we keep the tank at least half full, we have a choice of filling it or not filling it.

50. **A** This is the only logical conclusion.

Computer Operator Test Scale

50		
	SUPERIOR	Outstanding computer operational ability. Score indicates disciplined attention to rules and a high level of logic in problem solving.
45		
	EXCELLENT	Above-average operational ability, with close attention to details and a very logical thought process.
40		
	AVERAGE	Good computer operational ability. Score indicates a fairly logical thought process and the ability to follow rules and instructions most of the time.
35		
	CAPABLE	Score indicates that the individual definitely has the ability to operate a computer, but must pay greater attention to details and rules.
30		
	ADEQUATE	Individual has the basic intelligence and ability to operate a computer, but tends to ignore rules and is not always reasoning in a logical manner. Practice will correct much of this.
25		
	INSUFFICIENT	A score of less than 25 does not mean the individual is incapable of operating a computer. What it does mean is that he or she is very careless of details and of following rules. Such lack of attention will bring many difficulties. However, if these habits are corrected, the individual will certainly be able to operate a computer.
0		

Test Interpretation

The Computer Operator Test you just took was designed to test your current aptitudes in those areas of competency that are essential in the operation of a computer—namely, the precise following of all rules and procedures and a step-by-step logic in solving problems, and visualization of patterns and interconnections. The person who scrupulously follows all rules and thinks logically will be very successful in operating a computer. However, nothing can be taken for granted, and the individual cannot make assumptions the way we normally do in our everyday thinking process. Every detail and step must be observed in the operation of a computer. It must again be emphasized that a computer is only a machine, and it will do only what it is told to do. If even the simplest step—a period, a number, an instruction—is misplaced or overlooked, the machine will malfunction, or not even function at all. It is that simple.

One of the most common expressions in the computer world is GIGO, meaning garbage in, garbage out. This expression emphasizes that in computer operation the individual will get out of the machine exactly what he or she puts into it. To expect the computer to think and perform by itself would be as illogical as starting up your automobile and expecting it to drive itself without your direction and assistance. Just as with driving your automobile, you must direct the actions of the computer, and you must follow each and every rule—or it will not perform effectively.

The structure of the test follows the same general route to be followed in operating a computer.

First, the section on syntax rules tests aptitude for recognizing new language characters and following precise rules. You will have similar demands made upon you in the operation of a computer—specifically, using different characters and codes in detailed procedures.

The second section of the test—on problem analysis—examines ability to evaluate a given situation and proceed to a conclusion in a logical manner. You will go through a similar evaluation in using a computer to perform a specific task or tasks. In brief, you will order the computer, in a logical and step-by-step procedure, to complete some task or objective.

The third section of the test—procedure analysis—is a continuation of the testing of aptitude for logical thinking and progressive procedure, the same processes that are necessary in computer operation. The flow charts in the test are literally maps of the procedure or program a computer follows in handling a specific task or problem. Your analysis of the flow chart, again, is the same type of intellectual activity you must follow in operating a computer program. Both right-brain and left-brain activities contribute to success here.

Regardless of your score, rest assured that if you are of normal intelligence you can operate a computer. If your score on this test was lower than you would have liked, it does not mean you are incapable of operating a computer. What it indicates is that you are inclined to be more careless of details than you should be. And in the operation of a computer, those who are negligent of details—regardless of their level of intelligence or capability—will have difficulties in computer operation.

In general, since the test examines your current ability to follow precise rules and to think logically, the test score is a good indicator of how competent you will be in the early stages of operation of a computer. Computing, like reading and writing, is a skill that must be learned, and, of course, the more experience or practice one gains, the greater the level of competency.